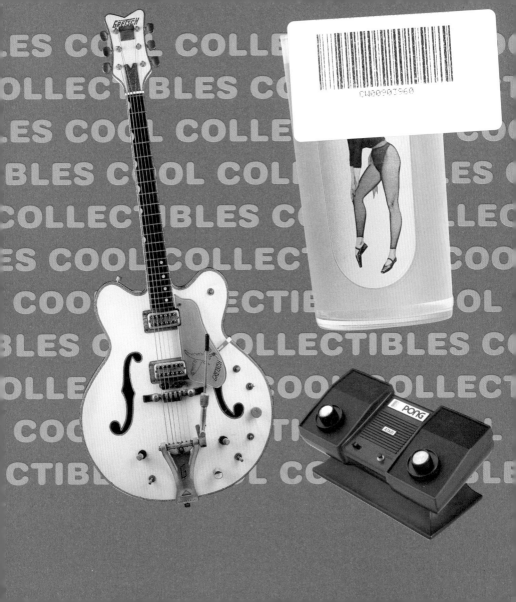

GRETSCH

PONG

MILLER'S

COOL
COLLECTIBLES

COOL
COLLECTIBLES

Dan Synge

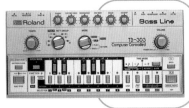

COOL COLLECTIBLES

Dan Synge

First published in Great Britain in 2004 by Miller's,
an imprint of Octopus Publishing Group Ltd,
2–4 Heron Quays, London E14 4JP

Miller's is a registered trademark of Octopus
Publishing Group Ltd

Senior Executive Editor	Anna Sanderson
Executive Art Editor	Rhonda Fisher
Senior Editor	Peter Taylor
Designer	Vicky Short
Proofreader	Kim Richardson
Indexer	Sandra Shotter
Production	Sarah Rogers
Special Photography	Steve Tanner

ISBN 1 84000 894 6

A CIP record for this book is available from the
British Library

Set in Swiss 721 BT
Produced by Toppan Printing Co., (HK) Ltd.
Printed and bound in China

PRICE RANGES
$ = Under £100 (Under $160)
$$ = £100–500 ($160–800)
$$$ = £500–1000 ($800–1600)
$$$$ = £1000–5000 ($1600–8000)
$$$$$ = Over £5000 (Over $8000)

CONTENTS

Armed with an appreciation of design, fashion, pop culture, and sport, a new breed of collector is making their presence felt in the once stuffy antiques world.

Luckily for them, a youth and consumer explosion has been in progress since the middle of the last century, and all kinds of fun and unusual collectibles have emerged to tempt the nostalgically inclined.

Top-drawer auction houses regularly hold high-profile sales of Sex Pistols artwork and James Bond memorabilia, while online traders and specialist dealers have wised up to American pulp novels, *Star Wars* toys, and "old skool" technology.

Rather than let go of our past obsessions, it is clear that we are putting entirely new values on them, and prices fetched by classic Corgi cars or vintage Nike sneakers bear this out.

So what makes an old inanimate object the ideal modern-day collectible? First it should be a one-off, totally unique in terms of concept, looks, and design. And if it oozes period charm, inspires everyone who sees it, or even has investment potential, then this won't do any harm either.

Collectibility aside, practically everything covered in this book has a quality that no-one has truly been able to define: cool. Everyone has their own idea of cool, but if it's a Jimi Hendrix guitar solo or the roar of a classic British motorbike, then this eclectic bunch of collectibles certainly fits the bill.

HOME HOME H
ME HOME HO
HOME HOME
E HOME HOM

HOME HOME HO
HOME HOM
HOME HOME H
HOME HOME

INTRODUCTION

Some collectibles are made for the domestic setting. Take electronic gadgets such as the television or the radio. We all know their true purpose: they're there to provide us with top-quality sound and vision. Yet if the appliance has something special about it – perhaps an unusual shape or never-been-seen-before colour – then this criterion goes swiftly out of the window.

Needless to say, the following home-based collectibles would enhance any pad. There are 1960s space-age televisions, stylish European phones, esoteric foreign film posters, and the sensational covers of pulp novels and ten-cent comics. There's even space for the humble classroom globe in the modern-day home, where new nestles comfortably next to retro or just plain old.

As well as blending in nicely with the Eames coffee table and the white shag-pile, these seemingly inanimate objects each have their own story to tell. The transistor radios, cocktail shakers, and match books that feature in the next few pages are more than mere relics of another age, they are the link between 20th-century commerce and some of pop culture's finest moments.

ELECTRONIC GADGETS

The arrival of VHS video, satellite, and digital services have all changed the way we use our television sets, but there is no stopping our addiction. If you are going to spend time in front of the magic rectangle, do it with a classic.

The Apollo Moon landings of 1969 attracted over 600 million viewers worldwide. Echoing the achievements of the "space age", product designers were drawn away from wood to cheaper, more adaptable materials such as plastic. Boxy TV designs gave way to globular or spherical shapes like Panasonic's TR-005, also known as "The Orbitel". Flying saucer-like with a tiny five-inch screen, it came with swivel base and impressive twin aerials.

JVC's take on the lunar landings was the Videosphere. A design from 1970, it came with a smoked acrylic visor that paid homage to a US astronaut's helmet. Grundig's "Super Colour" was one of the first remote-control televisions produced in the early 1970s. Unfortunately, it didn't take off and only 2,250 of these space-age relics were made. From Group Systems in the UK, the "Keracolor" led the new colour generation. Top-of-the-range models had an enormous 26-inch screen and cost a prohibitive £900 back in 1970.

As the decade progressed, Japanese manufacturers began exerting their grip on the electronic goods market. TV sets got smaller and a lot funkier, with increased portability reflecting a more mobile and individualistic society.

Invented by Nobel-winning research scientists at Bell Laboratories, the solid state transistor radio arrived in the late 1950s. Its handy size – ideal for a shirt or jean pocket – quickly came to symbolize youth rebellion and

01 Panasonic TR-005 Orbitel television. 1975. Ⓢ Ⓢ Ⓢ

02 Grundig Super Colour television. Early 1970s. Ⓢ Ⓢ Ⓢ Ⓢ

03 JVC Videosphere television. 1970. Ⓢ Ⓢ Ⓢ Ⓢ

04 Keracolor B-626 television. 1970. Ⓢ Ⓢ Ⓢ

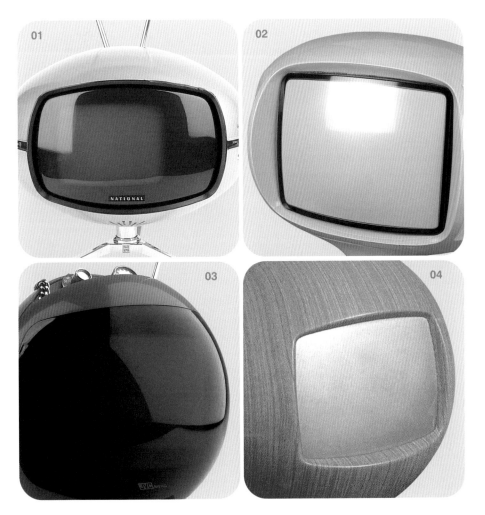

teenagers could tune into the latest rock 'n' roll stations away from the household, where the old valve radio still took pride of place.

American manufacturers Philco and Motorola produced some of the most stylish small radios of the period, but Regency's TR-1 claimed to be "The world's first pocket radio". Despite a $49.95 price tag (no small amount for 1954), sales were good. Models were sold in a mouth-watering array of colours; look out for meridian blue and lime "pearlescent".

Many pre-1963 American transistors had small triangular marks indented on the dial to show frequencies for emergency tuning in case of nuclear attack. The US government were wary of the fact that known frequencies could be used for guiding in Soviet missiles.

Slimmed-down sets that used smaller batteries, such as Sony's TR-63, appeared in the 1960s. The TR-63 was the first Japanese transistor made for export, and in America interest in this new "pocketable radio" was so great that a special JAL plane was chartered to fly stocks in.

05 Weltron catalogue from the late 1960s showing the range.

06 Weltron 2010 music centre with rare recordable 8 track. Late 1960s. $$

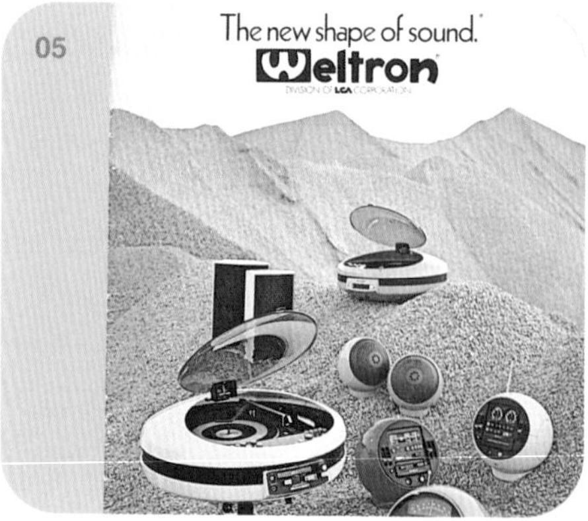

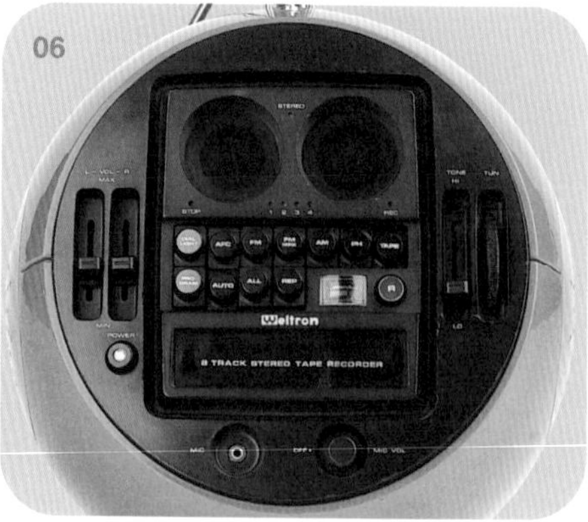

Another Japanese firm, National Panasonic, was responsible for the idiosyncratic R-72 radio, also known as the "Toot-a-Loop". It was designed so that pop fans could arrange its moulded plastic shell into a number of portable shapes.

For years man had to use the abacus or the slide rule (and occasionally his brain) when it came to mathematical conundrums. The personal electronic calculator came to the rescue in the early 1970s. Seemingly overnight the market was awash with futuristic-looking LEDs (light-emitting diodes) and LCDs (liquid crystal displays). A new executive toy had arrived.

Canon got in first with their 1970 "Pocketronic", even though it printed out calculations on thermal paper and was too bulky for most pockets. Two years later, however, Hewlett-Packard's HP-35 claimed to be the first hand-held scientific model, yet at a pricey $395 it was for boffins only.

British inventor Clive Sinclair brought out his Sinclair Executive model in the same year, which was priced at a more reasonable $79.95. Boasting

Plastic fantastic

In the late 1960s, Japan's Weltron fused electronics and moulded plastic to produce some of the most futuristic-looking home objects around. The Weltron 2001 was known as the "Space Ball" and functioned as both radio and eight-track player. The Weltron 2004 had an identical spherical cabinet but with cassette deck in place of the eight-track player. It came in white, red, or yellow. Vinyl lovers will be more taken by the Weltron 2007 hi-fi system. Hailed as "the new shape of sound", this ultimate bachelor pad accessory could be placed on a table or mounted on a pedestal.

slimmer design and showcasing an impressive red LED display, it became an instant design classic.

The next significant revolution came with credit-card sized, solar- powered models which came primarily from Japan. The Sharp EL-825, produced in 1981, featured a 76 x 50mm fold-up solar card and eight-digit LCD display. Just add batteries and switch on to enjoy retro number crunching.

✪ coolest buy Brionvega RR126

Both a music system and a groovy piece of 1960s home furniture, the RR126 was designed for Brionvega by Achille Castiglioni, creative force behind the Arco floor lamp and the Mezzadro tractor stool.

Intended as a "musical pet" with its very own face and ears, it ran on casters and had detachable speakers. It can be put together like a sideboard or mounted into a cube. It is available usually finished in white, red, and teak effect. Red is the rarest colour.

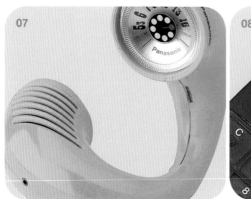

16-17 ELECTRONIC GADGETS

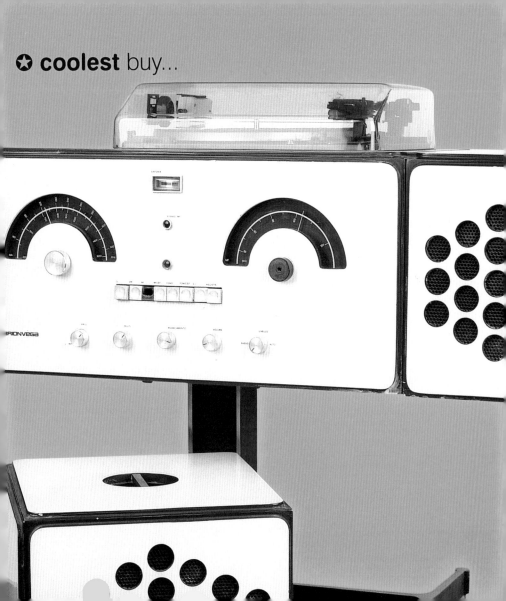

✪ **coolest** buy...

TELEPHONES

-->

Invented over 130 years ago, Alexander Graham Bell's telephone quickly became an essential business and domestic appliance. From early candlestick designs where the receiver was separate from the speaking microphone, telephones evolved into more solid-looking objects, moulded in Bakelite and, later, plastic casings.

Advances in telecommunications brought the telephone to just about every home in the West. The last few decades has seen a number of added innovations – answer machines, dial-up services, and cordless phones – yet all these have been eclipsed by our current obsession, the mobile.

The 700 Series comes from an era when landline devices still set the style. Replacing the distinctly pre-war looking 300 Series that had a standard black finish, Bakelite casing, and drawer in base, the 700 Series was the first plastic phone to be made in Britain. Available in "six colours and black", it became an instant hit with consumers. Today, the 700 is still a good buy and can be easily adapted to today's networks.

The luxury lightweight Trimphone was the GPO's response to the global trend in dinky plastic designer phones. TRIM stands for "tone ringing illuminated model". Designed by Martin Rowlands in 1966, it had a glow-in-the-dark fluorescent dial and a distinct, high-pitched ring tone.

Early models had dials which were later suspected of having radioactive qualities, so push-button versions replaced them in 1981. The Trimphone was produced in a mouthwatering range of colours, including brown/cream and olive green/beige from Lord Linley's "Snowdon Range".

01 Ericafons. Late 1950s. $

02 Grillo ("cricket") phone. 1965. $$

03 Trubphone. 1970s. $

04 Trimphone. 1970s. $

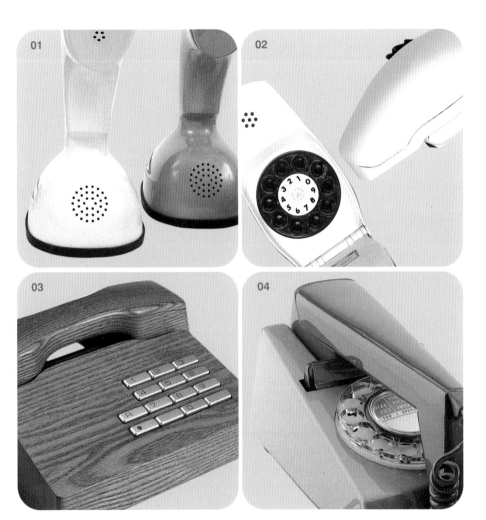

✪ American Western Electric 500 Series telephone. 1950s. [$]

By the time the Trimphone was launched, Europe was already way ahead in plastic phone design. The Swedish Ericafon (also known as the Cobra phone) was first produced by L.M. Ericsson in 1957. Designed by Ralph Lysell and Hugo Blomberg using the latest micro-electronic components, it was the first ever one-piece phone. The cleverest feature is the dial which is located at the base.

The Grillo is another design classic, this time by Marco Zanuso and Richard Sapper, who were also responsible for Brionvega's Algol and Doney portable televisions. The Grillo ("cricket" in Italian) shows the same plastic/organic approach and has a clever dial mechanism. It sits crouched on a desk, or when ringing folds open like a modern-day cellphone.

From the design-conscious Swiss the Trubphone fitted the vogue for pine, rosewood, or teak interiors when it appeared briefly in the 1970s. Shaped like an early computer keyboard, it featured sleek push-button dials worthy of a reception desk of a five-star Geneva hotel.

✪ **coolest buy** 500 Series

Watch any American movie from the 1950s or 1960s in which a phone conversation takes place, and the chances are it will be on a 500 Series.

Most often black but sometimes light grey and blue, they were introduced in 1949 by Western Electric. Innovations from designer Henry Dreyfuss included sans-serif lettering outside the round finger dial to reduce chances of misdialling. At the time, demand was so high for this new model that disappointed customers customised their old 302 models for a similar look.

This classic phone was much imitated across the world (most obviously by the British 700 Series) and stayed in production until the mid 1980s. Early models have metal finger dials while later models have them in clear plastic.

BAR AND COCKTAIL

The cocktail shaker is a lasting and highly collectible symbol for the Jazz Age, during which no self-respecting high roller or his flapper would consider kicking off an evening with anything other than a dry martini.

A necessity at the Prohibition-era "speakeasy", these sterling silver bar accessories came in a variety of forms, reflecting either the technical achievements of the age (skyscrapers, aeroplanes, Zeppelins, etc) or contemporary style. A popular shaker of the time took the form of a penguin dressed in fashionable bow tie and tuxedo.

With their pleasurable alcoholic hit and incorporation of vogue-ish tipples such as gin and French vermouth, cocktails soon caught on outside the smart New York hotels they originated from, and inspired by the Hollywood movies of the time, people began to host their own cocktail parties. Soon practically everybody was able to enjoy happy hour.

During the 1930s, shakers were mass produced, more often than not in the affordable, universal style of Art Deco. Out went the pure solid silver look, and in came a range of new materials including Bakelite and coloured glass. One of the most collectible shakers from the period is a ruby glass and chrome affair shaped like a woman's leg, dubbed the "Shake A Leg".

With the exception of Rik's Bar in the film *Casablanca*, World War Two halted the consumption of Manhattans and whisky sours, yet cocktail culture returned with a vengeance in the 1950s. This time, however, stylish pre-war shakers were beginning to be replaced by the electric blender.

01 Silver penguin design by Emil Schuelke for Napier. 1937–41. $$$

02 Glass fire extinguisher by West Virginia Glass Company. 1934–41. $$$

03 Bakelite "The Master Incolor". 1935–40. $$

04 Generic decorated glass shaker from the USA. 1950s. $$

THIRST EXTINGUISHER

REQUIRED BY LAW
TO BE PUT IN CONVENIENT SPOT

IN EMERGENCIES CHARGE
WITH INGREDIENTS SHAKE

DRY MARTINI
DRY GIN
VERMOUTH
ITALIAN VERMOUTH
ORANGE BITTER
ICE

Bars themselves had come to the home. Areas where pre- and after-dinner drinking took place were known as "roc rooms". Finished in exotic bamboo or the latest materials such as Formica, home bars displayed the sort of cocktail accessories (plastic pineapple ice buckets, Tiki-style ashtrays, decorative drinking glasses) that today fall firmly in the kitsch camp.

In the 1950s and 1960s, manual shakers were often made in glass and were printed with colourful, garish designs. Popular themes included roosters and pink elephants, although ones emblazoned with classic cocktail recipes were arguably the most practical.

Complete cocktail drinking sets featuring matching glasses and serving trays are also highly collectible, although increasingly hard to find. The definitive set is the "Manhattan", designed by streamlining guru Norman Bel Geddes, also known for working on amphibian airliners and flying cars. Brass or chrome versions from the 1930s made by Gorham or Chase are also worth looking out for.

05 Pineapple ice bucket with glass liner. 1950s. $

06 Playboy Club memorabilia. 1960s. $

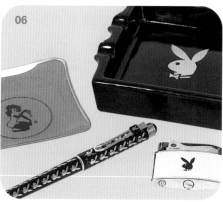

24-25 BAR AND COCKTAIL

When it comes to buying glasses on their own, bear in mind that a set is more valuable than an individual item. Prices are further enhanced if the set comes with its original packaging.

Swizzle sticks (those coloured plastic things placed by bartenders in a full cocktail glass) go down like Singapore slings at happy hour among bar ephemera collectors around the world. Invented by one Jay Sindler in 1935 after wondering how to extract an olive from his dry martini, the swizzle has gone on to endorse drink brands, hotels, airlines, casinos, and nightclubs.

Swizzle sticks can be both a graphic relic of legendary drinking establishments or simply a souvenir of a great night out. Trader Vic's palm trees or top Las Vegas casinos such as the Golden Nugget rank as the some of the most wanted plastic swizzles around, although serious collectors might also be tempted to invest in earlier wood or blown glass versions.

Playboy international

In its heyday, the Playboy Club had branches in at least 35 cities including London, Osaka, and Manila. A place where cigar-chomping males played blackjack whilst being served cocktails by glamorous bunny girls, the first club opened in Chicago in 1960.

From these now long-closed down clubs there is plenty for the collector to get their hands on, as many members at the time admit to pocketing practically anything that featured the famous bunny logo. Choose from glassware, ashtrays, cocktail swizzle sticks, and match books.

✪ **coolest buy** Match books

Both a cheap promotional tool and saviour for the lighter-less smoker, the match book first came into use in the 1890s. One of the first companies to take advantage of this new form of advertising was Wrigley's chewing gum; "Had any lately?" ran the slogan.

Today match books are seen as a walking, talking piece of 1940s or 1950s Americana. Imagine Frank Sinatra strolling out of the Sands Hotel with his Rat Pack buddies circa 1958. Chances are he'd have stuck his first cigarette with the aid of an embossed match book picked up from the Copa Room bar. Made with front, rear, and bottom phosphorous strike strips, match books have always been a cool alternative to the European-style matchbox.

Collectors today have little interest in what's beneath the flip-up cover. The most sought-after designs are cover girls, casinos, and Hawaii, closely followed by Holiday Inns and American motels.

07 Plastic whistle cocktail stirrers. 1950s. $

08 Keyhole glass (nude on back). 1950s. Set of four: $

✪ **US and UK match books from hotels, bars, and restaurants. 1950s–60s.** $

07

08

✪ **coolest** buy...

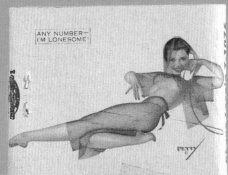

MOVIE POSTERS

Originally intended as a highly disposable method of street advertising, vintage posters have become highly collectible of late. Whether depicting films, art, or politics, they look great when framed and put up around the home.

Like movie-goers, film poster collectors go in for genres such as sci-fi, gangsters, 60s Counterculture, and Bond. B-movie posters date from an era when America was feeling more than a little vulnerable from the threat of Soviet invasion and when film audiences were deserting movie theatres for the domestically positioned television. So-called to distinguish it from the studios' higher budget productions, the B-movie was a none-too-subtle quick-fix entertainment with tons of gimmickry.

The 1950s was an era for drive-in theatres, 3-D glasses, "Strangloscope", and wild hyperbole: "Teenage hoodlums from another world go on a horrendous ray-gun rampage", said the poster for *Teenagers From Outer Space* (1959).

With dubious performances and production values alongside promotional material that abandoned all notions of good taste, the movies made no pretensions to high art, yet 50 years later their value certainly warrants reappraisal.

Invaders From Mars (1953) and *Forbidden Planet* (1956) tapped into the craze for anything connected to space adventure, while *The Incredible Shrinking Man* (1957) imagined a nightmarish world in which man is reduced to the size of a match book.

Poster for *The Godfather*. 1972.
Ⓢ Ⓢ

Stylistically, B-movie poster artwork delivers its remit to get audiences away from the TV and into the movie theatre, and this appears to be having the same effect on poster collectors today.

James Bond is another poster favourite, with Ian Fleming's enduring secret agent continuing his celluloid adventures almost half a century since he first appeared on the big screen.

Aesthetically and stylistically, however, it is the early films starring Sean Connery, and later Roger Moore, which arouse most interest. *Goldfinger* (1964) was the third of Bond's screen appearances. Designed by Robert Brownjohn, the standard promotional poster portrays a more swaggering version of the brand. "James Bond Is Back In Action!" roars the strap line to the one- and three-sheet versions. It wouldn't be the last time, either.

As one would expect from an industry as complex as the movie business, printing quality and poster size vary a great deal. The standard

02 Poster for *Forbidden Planet*. 1956. $$$$$

03 Poster for *Vertigo*. 1958. $$$$

04 Poster for *Goldfinger*. 1964. $$$$

The art of Saul Bass

Film poster collectors are often led by genre or preferred actors and directors. In only a few instances does the poster designer have an influence, and in Saul Bass's case, his influence is supreme. Starting out as a designer in New York, Bass began his Hollywood career overseeing the graphic look of Otto Preminger's *Carmen Jones* (1954) and later *The Man With The Golden Arm* (1955) and *Anatomy of a Murder* (1959). Bass's collaborations with Alfred Hitchcock such as *Vertigo* (1958) and *North By North West* (1959) demonstrate his much-imitated geometric style, identifiable by key motifs, bold colours, and respect for space.

American film poster size is the "one sheet", which measures 27 x 41 inches. Vintage posters come in "half sheets" (made for cinema lobby display), "three sheets", and sometimes billboard-sized "six sheets". The British standard size is known as the quad, while a smaller size – used for street walls or for pasting on to the side of buses – is referred to as "double crown".

Experienced collectors will be aware of the amount of reproductions on the market. Here's a tip: generally speaking, posters produced before the late 1980s were folded into sections at the printers. After that, posters were rolled up and distributed in tubes.

○ **coolest buy** Cuban film posters

After the communist revolution of 1959, Fidel Castro set up the Cuban Film Institute (ICAIC) so that home-grown films and documentaries could be shown all over the island.

An antidote to pre-revolutionary Hollywood offerings, the new Cuban film movement dealt with worthier and more relevant themes, among them salsa, ballet, and politics.

Posters, produced on old-fashioned silk screens at Havana's ICAIC workshop, reflected this change. Borrowing from Pop Art, comics, and the Polish graphic style, they look as fresh and vibrant as when they were first made.

Although artists like Eduardo Munoz Bachs (*Vampiros en la Habana*) and Antonio Perez (*Frenesi*) have hardly been acknowledged for their work, collectors pay high prices for 1960s and 1970s originals. Newly screen-printed film posters can still be bought for as little as $5 direct from the ICAIC or the foyer of Havana's famous Yara cinema.

○ Poster for the Cuban release of the 1967 Japanese film *Ai to shi no kiroku* (English title: *The Heart of Hiroshima*). 1969. ⓢ

32-33 MOVIE POSTERS

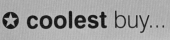
✪ **coolest** buy...

film japonés en cinemascope dirección: koreyoshi kurahara
con: sayuri yoshinaga / tetsuya watari
LOS AMANTES DE HIROSHIMA

GLOBES

---→

Spherical-shaped maps have been around since European explorers went out to discover the world. Once a geographical, nautical, and educational necessity, the stand-up globe is now desirable as a decorative object.

Old globes have political and historical appeal and collectors especially like ones that depict vast empires or countries and principalities that have long been merged into larger states.

Modern vintage table globes (1930s to 1960s) vary considerably. They can be spun under a semi-circular meridian ring (usually in silver chrome and marked with degrees of latitude) or are simply mounted on a base. Sometimes they rest on a simple wooden cradle mount. Surfaces are made of papier-mâché or tin, while map sections (known in globe parlance as "the gore") usually depict oceans as blue, although black is also common.

The information gleaned from the average vintage globe might be anything from international air routes to the relief topography of the Andes. Replogle's mid-1950s "Surprise" table globe even opened up to reveal concave northern and southern celestial hemispheres, while in the late 1960s there was a fashion for producing moon globes that enabled school kids to chart the lunar surface and, of course, the Apollo 11 and 12 landing sites. Globes that light up in the dark are especially collectible.

Look for globes made in America by Rand McNally, Weber Costello, and Replogle. Avoid scratched and dented models and be sure that they spin properly before parting with your money. Expect to pay around £20 for educational tin versions to £400 for light-up models with decorative stands.

✪ Replogle Wonder World globe. 1950s.
Ⓢ Ⓢ

✪ coolest buy...

✪ coolest buy Wonder World

In 1930, Chicago firm Replogle set out to supply the world with "a globe in every home". Still manufacturing them over 70 years later, their biggest globe size is 32 inches in diameter, although the standard size is 12 inches.

Made for educational purposes by Chicago firm Replogle in the 1950s, this 10-inch globe features a mounted hour dial and metal base that stores a book, *The World is Yours*, which contains educational information, such as how to use latitude and longitude, and games. The cartography is simple but this is more than made up by its illustrations of international air routes, Eskimos, and a penguin.

PULP FICTION

With their racy kitsch covers and questionable literary content, pulp novels never pretended to be anything other than a ten-cent throwaway read for the man-on-the-move. The typical pulp novel featured a hard-boiled detective, a mystery blonde, and a whole lot of smoky bars and neon-lit alleyways.

Writers of the genre (which was popular up until the early 1960s) included Raymond Chandler, Dashiell Hammett, and *Naked Lunch* author William Burroughs, who was then masquerading under the name Bill Lee.

Collectors are usually led by genre, be it crime fiction, sci-fi, or juvenile delinquency. Cover art with its provocative depiction of women also draws interest. Although produced cheaply and quickly at the time, original cover artwork now attracts premium prices.

The most highly sought-after books are first-print PBOs (paperback originals). It's worth scouring flea markets and junk shops for these, as well as map-backed copies (issues with maps attached to the back cover to show where the mystery took place) and Bantam LAs, which were originally sold from vending machines at subway stations.

Due to the large numbers of copies published, there is a lot pulp fiction still around today, many with wonderfully sensationalist titles such as *Swamp Girl* and *Vixen Hollow*. Unfortunately mint condition covers are getting rarer; many were actually torn off by readers who were too ashamed to let their wives see them.

Ian Fleming's debonair secret agent James Bond first appeared in *Casino Royale*, published in hardback by Jonathan Cape in 1953. By 1955,

01 Chris Wheatley, *Red Ice.* Published by Barrington Gray Ltd, Essex. 1950s. $

02 Ian Fleming, *For Your Eyes Only.* Published by Pan Books. 1962. $

03 Robert E. Howard, *The Blonde Goddess of Bal-Sagoth.* Published by Avon. 1950s. $

RED ICE

ACE OF GANGSTER AUTHORS

CHRIS WHEATLEY

1/6

GREAT PAN

FOR YOUR EYES ONLY

Ian Fleming

MINAS
PERICOLO
DI
MORTE

Oval.

EXECUTIONER!
SPY-CATCHER!
Spectacular
exploits of
Britain's agent

JAMES BOND SECRET

6

AVON

Fantasy

35¢

READER No. 12

THE BLONDE GODDESS OF
BAL-SAGOTH by Robert E. Howard

his adventures had begun in paperback, courtesy of Pan, who were to publish popular thrillers by John Le Carre and Gavin Lyall.

The cover of Pan's *Casino Royale* was the first graphic interpretation of Bond, in this instance wearing the now familiar bow tie and tux at the gaming table. Copies fetch up to £140 today, or around £70 for his other Pan adventures like *Moonraker* and *For Your Eyes Only*.

✪ coolest buy Larry Kent

Larry Kent was the private dick hero of over 400 novels and "one shilling" novelettes. He started off as a press hack in New York, but relocated to Australia where he became a detective. His adventures, which have great titles such as *Lady, You're Loaded!* and *Dame Die Hard*, also take place in Los Angeles, Cuba, and Berlin. No-one would pick up a Larry Kent today for the writing – the covers are far more interesting – but you can be sure that wherever he goes, Kent keeps up his hobby, "Watching the blondes go by."

04 Back cover of Dashiel Hammett's *Blood Money*. Published by Dell. 1940s. Ⓢ

05 Back cover of Baynard Kendrick, *Death Knell*. Published by Dell. 1946. Ⓢ

✪ Larry Kent books. Published by the Cleveland Publishing Co, Australia. 1950s. Ⓢ

✪ **coolest** buy...

COMICS

Comics are no longer just for kids. Prices for 30- and 40-year-old examples have reached heights that only the superheroes inside could appreciate.

Collectors choose characters or titles that take them directly back to their bubble gum-popping, catapult-firing schooldays, which perhaps explains a continued interest in childhood favourites such as *The Eagle*, *MAD* magazine, and *The Beano.*

Other than that, vintage comic lovers are guided by era. Superman's 1938 debut in DC's Action Comics marks the beginning of the so-called "golden age", a period which also spawned Captain America and Gotham City's masked vigilante, Batman. The famous "caped crusader" created by Bob Kane has starred in countless screen and television incarnations, but was first seen in *Detective Comics* issue 27 in May 1939. Sales of Batman comics tripled after the appearance of his youthful sidekick, Robin.

After World War Two comics turned to horror, crime, and romance. In the 1950s they suffered a moral backlash when US Senate hearings linked comics to child delinquency. The subsequent Comics Code Authority (CCA) aimed to tone down the violent content of children's comics, and a CCA mark was stamped on all approved publications. Sales slumped and many talented comic book artists and writers fell by the wayside.

Good things were round the corner, however. The "silver age" spans the early 1960s through to the 1970s, a period in which DC's publishing rivals Marvel began to dominate the comic book world. Classic Marvel creations such as The Fantastic Four, Spider Man, and The Incredible Hulk owed

01 ***Batman.*** **Number 84. 1954.** [$][$]

02 ***Superman.*** **G-84, number 239. 1971.** [$]

03 ***Fantastic Four.*** **Number 86. 1969.** [$]

04 ***Spiderman.*** **Number 143. 1975.** [$]

01

02

03

04

everything to the storytelling genius of Stan Lee and his illustrators Jack Kirby and Steve Ditko.

Before buying an old comic, check for fingerprints, tears, and spine damage, all of which slash the value. As a general rule, first issues such as the first *Action Comic* or first *Captain America* arouse most interest, but if your early superheroes were Dan Dare or Dennis the Menace...

05 *The Beano*. Number 652. 1955. $

06 *The Dandy*. Number 458. 1950. $

✪ *2000 AD*. Numbers 18 and 56. 1977/8. $

✪ coolest buy 2000 AD

Born during the height of punk rock in 1977, *2000 AD* was the direct descendant of UK sci-fi comics such as *The Eagle* and *TV21*. But with gritty urban futurescapes reminiscent of late-1970s Britain, and characters that had a nice line in British deadpan, the tone couldn't have been more different.

Judge Dredd, the tough Mega-City One lawman devised by John Wagner (story) and Carlos Ezquerra (art), proved to be its most popular creation, and he was soon attracting a whole new fanbase in the US.

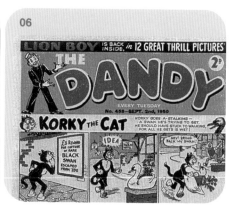

PROG. 18

Prog 59   8 APR 78

2000 A.D.

9P
EARTH
MONEY

MEGA CITY
BEWARE—
THE JUDGE
IS BACK!

IN ORBIT
EVERY
MONDAY

SHIRT OFFER!

MAGAZINES

Old magazines appeal on many levels, but their design, artwork, and social historical value usually come first.

US *Esquire* and *Playboy* set the standard in magazine publishing by commissioning some of the best writers and designers of their time, and their hip, knowing style is much imitated today.

Playboy, Hugh Hefner's men's lifestyle bible, first hit the news stands over half a century ago. Adorned with cover star and "Sweetheart of the Month" Marilyn Monroe, it had an initial print run of just 70,000 copies.

The pipe-smoking, pyjama-wearing Hef may have been uncertain about his latest venture but the *Playboy* philosophy was already firmly in place. "We enjoy mixing cocktails," he wrote in his first editorial, "... putting a little mood music on the phonograph and inviting in a female acquaintance for a quiet discussion on Picasso, Nietzsche, jazz, and sex." Copies of *Playboy* issue one have traded hands for up to £350,000. After that, they go down appreciably as print-runs later ran into the millions.

The late-1960s counterculture eventually dated sophisticated man-about-town titles and heralded in a host of low-cost, close-to-the-scene publications, of which *Rolling Stone* has been the most enduring. Started by Jan Wenner in 1967 in San Francisco, it aimed to capture the music and attitude of the 1960s hippy generation. Early copies were printed on cheap serrated-edged newspaper and featured lengthy articles by the likes of Lester Bangs and Hunter S. Thompson, who wrote his infamous "Fear and Loathing in Las Vegas" article for issue 95, published in November 1971.

01 *Playboy*. September 1971. $

02 *Rolling Stone*. September 1975. $

03 *Interview*. 1980s. $

04 *The Face*. December 1987. $

01

ENTERTAINMENT FOR MEN

SEPTEMBER 1971 · ONE DOLLAR

PLAYBOY

02

SM14170

SEPTEMBER 11th, 1975 / ISSUE NO. 195

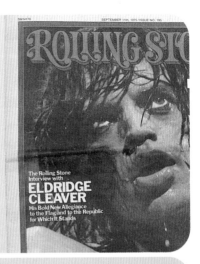

ROLLING STO

The Rolling Stone
Interview with
**ELDRIDGE
CLEAVER**
His Bold New Allegiance
to the Flag and to the Republic
for Which It Stands

03

Interview

$2.00

04

THE FACE

BOB'S YOUR UNCLE

DE NIRO
DELIVERS

Covers invariably featured the hottest bands of the moment. Beatles and Bob Dylan covers are especially sought after today.

Andy Warhol's *Interview*, launched in the more glamour-minded 1970s, was one of the first magazines to pick up on the cult of modern celebrity. It was essential reading for the New York Studio 54 set, who more often than not appeared inside its colourful matt pages. The page format was a whopping 10.5 x 6 inches allowing airbrushed cover stars such as Goldie Hawn and Grace Jones maximum exposure on news stands.

Music and cult fashion were first combined in glossy, monthly form when *The Face* appeared in 1980. This streetwise London-centric style mag designed by Neville Brody was the perfect antidote to the rock "inkies" of the late 1970s and helped propel the careers of Culture Club, Madonna, and Duran Duran, all of whom appeared on the cover. Issue number one, featuring the Specials and The Clash, is worth around £100 today.

✪ coolest buy 1960s Esquire

Blending razor sharp copy with cool, eye-catching photography and illustration, *Esquire* has been mirroring the interests of the American male since the 1930s. In its early days, it published writers of the calibre of F. Scott Fitzgerald and Ernest Hemingway. The literary tradition continued into the 1960s when it helped pioneer the "New Journalism" of Tom Wolfe and Norman Mailer.

Equally as groundbreaking were the covers designed by George Lois who dared to have Andy Warhol drowning in a tin of Campbell's soup (May 1969) and boxer Muhammad Ali tied up and shot by arrows (April 1968). With its high style sensibilities and often irreverent take on politics, *Esquire* truly managed to capture the spirit of the 1960s.

✪ *Esquire.*
April 1968. $

46-47 MAGAZINES

Esquire

APRIL 1968
PRICE $1

THE MAGAZINE FOR MEN

EVERLAST

The Passion of Muhammad Ali

PACKAGING

---→

Never actually meant to be something that people hold onto or store in an ordered manner, product packaging is becoming an increasingly popular area of collecting.

Brands singled out for most attention are Coca-Cola (bottles, key rings, glasses), Michelin (enamel garage signs, tins), and Guinness (anything from beer mats to metal trays). However, you don't have to follow the corporate big hitters if you are starting a collection of packaging or old advertising ephemera.

For those nostalgic for a glimpse of their own childhood, how about crisp, sweet, or ice cream wrappers? The 1960s and 1970s were a golden age for frozen ices with lollies like Fab, Zoom, and Orbit inspired by characters from the popular *Thunderbirds* TV show and its space-age puppet spin-offs *Joe 90* and *Captain Scarlet*.

Makers Lyons Maid continued to respond to the popular culture of the day with Space 1999 and Crime Squad, whilst rivals Wall's gave us Kinky ("an ice cream lolly with sugar strands") and the multi-flavoured Funny Faces.

Sweet manufacturing was an equally hard-fought battleground and children were faced with a dazzling array of goodies at the sweet shop. Today, names like Spangles, Curly Wurly, and Amazin' Raisin Bar are more likely to crop up in nostalgic pub conversations than in the corner shop.

Considering the unfashionability of smoking today, collecting the cigarette packets of yesteryear is a surprisingly popular hobby. In the US

01 Fab ice lolly wrapper. Late 1960s. Ⓢ

02 Orbit ice lolly wrapper. Late 1960s. Ⓢ

03 Kinky ice lolly wrapper. Late 1960s. Ⓢ

04 Zoom ice lolly wrapper. Late 1960s. Ⓢ

01

Lyons Maid

fab

FREE PICTURE CARD INSIDE

02

Lyons Maid

ORBIT

The big ice-cream on a stick.

03

Walls

Kinky

ICE CREAM LOLLY
CONTAINS NON-MILK FAT
WITH SUGAR STRANDS

04

Lyons Maid

ZOOM

FREE JOE 90 BADGE OFFER

collectors look for packets that are unopened, whereas European collectors prefer empty packets. Collections can be ordered into a number of themes such as era, flavour, or country of origin.

Early cigarette packs highlight the perceived glamour or even the health-giving qualities of the habit. Long-forgotten 1940s US brand Toppers featured a top-hatted gent in front of Manhattan's skyline, while a pre-war Indian brand, Football Cigarettes, had packets that depicted a game in full flow. Who said smoking was bad for you?

Another unhealthy habit, eating fast food, has led to the widespread hobby of collecting fast food memorabilia. Coffee cups, burger wrappers, even napkins are swallowed up by these collectors, although promotional giveaways attract the most interest on the market.

US chain Burger Chef was the first to introduce the idea back in the mid 1970s. Their *Star Wars* Land Speeder, made from a paper fold-out tray, preceded the first McDonald's Happy Meal by at least a year.

05 Spangles wrapper. 1950s. ⓢ

06 Texan Bar wrapper. 1970s. ⓢ

50-51 PACKAGING

Happy Meal items became instant collectibles and fast food collectors snap up anything from the giveaway toys to the boxes themselves. Due to the global nature of the company, there are infinite variations available, which makes it a challenge to complete collections. McDonald's Disney promotions are the most popular of all.

While it has been known for people to collect items from fast food giants such as Burger King and Wendy's, the Ronald McDonald motif exerts the most influence on the world of fast food collecting. Over the years the corporate clown and his famous yellow arches have found their way onto tumblers, plates, alarm clocks, and lunch boxes.

For a more off-the-wall approach to product packaging, why not scour the shelves of foreign supermarkets? Some collect the packaging of funny-sounding continental brands. Examples include Grany Maniac, a chocolate bar from France, or Bonka, a brand of Spanish coffee. It's certainly a fun and original way of livening up a rainy day on that next holiday abroad.

Vote for the PEZident

Pez – the plastic candy dispenser with the interchangeable head – has been a favourite with children and adults alike for over 50 years. The dispensers and their fruit-flavoured capsules originated in Austria and were an instant hit in 1950s USA, but it was licensed character heads, with well-known faces from Disney, Star Wars, and Asterix, that really propelled the Pez cult. Roughly 300 different heads (feet weren't added until the 1980s) have appeared over the years. There are collectors all over the world, as well as Pez conventions, museums, collectors clubs, and even a company PEZident.

✪ **coolest buy** Men's perfume

Grooming for the 1970s male was a serious business. While attitudes remained macho, moustaches and medallions abounded and hair grew well past jumbo-sized collars. A dab or two of sniff didn't go amiss either.

Fabergé launched Brut 33 aftershave with the help of top British sports celebrities Henry Cooper, Barry Sheene, and Kevin Keegan. Other products in the 1970s bathroom cabinet included Denim, Blue Stratos, Pagan Man, and the hi-kicking, irresistible-to-the-ladies Hai Karate. The latter tapped into the mid-1970s craze for oriental martial arts and the stylish black, red, and white bottles came with a self-defence guide to keeping "the birds" at bay.

Traditionalists were more likely to have stuck with Old Spice, a fragrance made by Shulton Inc. since the late 1930s. The famous white containers were first introduced in 1948 and were based on antique apothecary bottles. Today collectors pay good money for Old Spice shaving mugs, originally pottery-made but later mass-produced in glass.

07 Pair of Walt Disney plastic Pez holders. 1960–70. $

08 Rare gold plastic Pez ray gun. Late 1950s/early 1960s. $$$

✪ **Assorted aftershaves. 1970s.** $

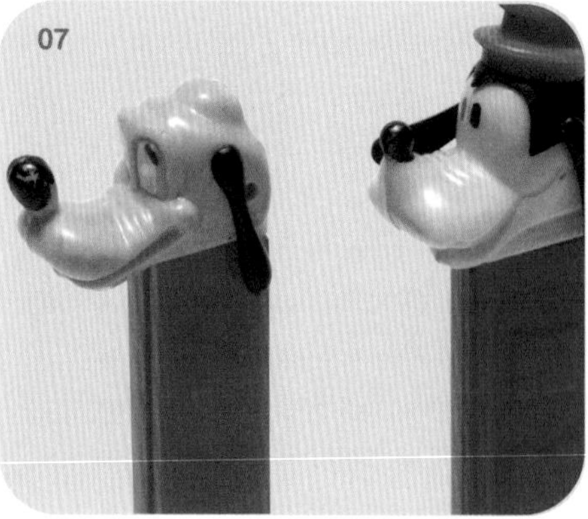

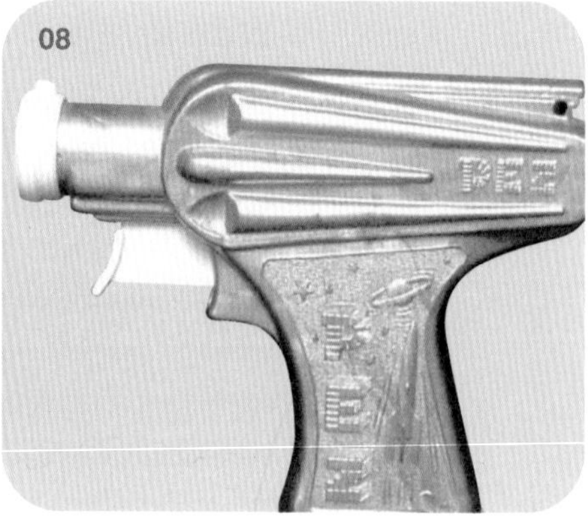

✪ **coolest** buy...

Old Spice
AFTER SHAVE LOTION

HAI *KARATE*
AFTER SHAVE LOTION

BRUT 33

FABERGÉ

BRUT 33

FABERGÉ INC.
Iver, Bucks., England.
LONDON PARIS
NEW YORK TORONTO
MILAN MUNICH
100 ml
ref E80991-026

AFTER SHAVE

Old Spice
AFTER SHAVE LOTION

BRUT
33
AFTER SHAVE

PLAY PLAY PLAY
PLAY PLAY PL
AY PLAY PLAY
PLAY PLAY PL

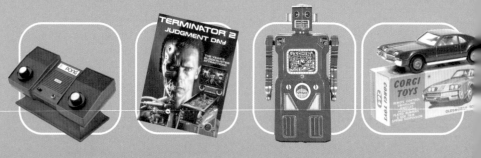

PLAY PLAY PL
AY PLAY PLAY
PLAY PLAY PL
AY PLAY PLAY

INTRODUCTION

In the world of collectibles, leisure opens up a whole lot of possibilities. Our forebears may have missed the fun of computer games and digital cameras, but they would never have complained about the things that entertained them.

From fiercely contested board games brought out at Christmas to early computer games and classic American pinball machines, the vintage games room fuses high concentration levels with a barrage of flashing bulbs and dot-matrix displays.

With old toy cupboards also having a clear out, there are rich pickings for adult baby boomers with credit cards and a continued obsession with robots, ray guns, or *Star Wars*.

Replica die-cast vehicles that would have once hogged the play room scrap yard now trade hands for prices that almost match their full-size metal counterparts.

Hobbyists of all eras have gravitated consistently towards a more complex invention, the camera. Fortunately, the Leicas and Rolleis favoured by previous generations of photographers continue to live side-by-side with their modern-day equivalents. Let play commence...

PINBALL MACHINES

--→

The game of choice amongst 1950s rockers, invariably holding court in some sleazy coffee bar, pinball is one of the ultimate man-versus-machine challenges in all its nudge, tilt, and multi-play glory.

Although originally intended for arcade and bar use, the machines are increasingly wanted for the domestic games room. Collectors see them as a fun way to unwind after a hard day at the office or as objects of artistic or historical value. Whether you choose to specialize in era, manufacturer, or game theme, the pinball machine stands out as a classic working piece of 20th-century Americana.

Pinball comes from the old pastime of bagatelle and first caught on during the 1930s, yet the "golden age" of pinball is thought to be the 1950s when gaudy artwork, whizz-round score reels, and flipper-style bumpers came into use.

Driven by manufacturers Gottlieb, Williams, Bally, and others, based almost exclusively in Chicago, USA, pinball technology quickly caught up with the needs of its quick-fingered punters.

The earliest machines were so easy to abuse that manufacturers came up with the now ubiquitous tilt mechanism. Flippers first appeared in 1947 on Gottlieb's "Humpty Dumpty", extra-ball games came in during the 1960s, while dot-matrix displays were a feature of pinball machines in the 1990s.

Often accused of being a cover for illegal gambling, coin-op pinball has had its run-ins with the authorities over the years. In 1942 pinball was

Gottlieb Lady Luck. 1954. $$$

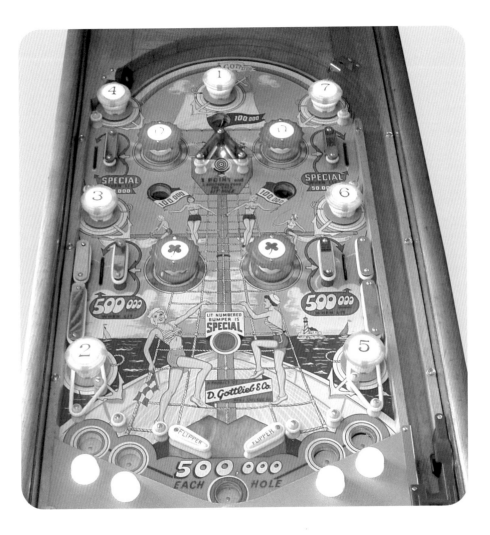

outlawed in New York, a ban which lasted until 1976 and was celebrated by the city's mayor smashing rows of pinball machines for the benefit of press photographers. Other US cities affected by the pinball ban were Los Angeles and, amazingly, Chicago.

Fuelled by 1950s revivalism and The Who's rock opera *Tommy* – "From Soho down to Brighton I must have played them all" ran the lyrics to "Pinball Wizard" – the 1970s pinball craze left us with some of the last classic pre-digital machines, among them "Captain Fantastic", "Evel Knievel", and "Kiss".

Solid state electronic pinball games with their multi-play facilities, wide bodies, and impressive digital score displays appeared in the late 1970s. Bally produced the Hugh Hefner-endorsed "Playboy" (1978) complete with built-in wolf whistle, while Williams's "Gorgar Speaks" (1979) is believed to be the first talking pinball game with its "Me Gorgar, Beat Me" taunt.

02 Gottlieb Humpty Dumpty. 1947. $$$$

03 Gottlieb Flipper. 1960. $$$$

In the 1980s, the ricocheting silver ball faced tough competition from the emerging video games market. If video was killing the radio star, then video games were about to bump off the pinball wizard.

While production in Chicago slowed down, versions of classic games were starting to appear in France, Spain, and Italy. Games made during the short-lived 1990s pinball boom are particularly collectible today. While they admittedly lack the charm of their "golden age" forebears, they demonstrate pinball machine technology at its peak, with sampled movie catchphrases and dot-matrix displays included.

Some collectors are interested primarily in the artwork that goes into a machine. Before the 1970s, playfields (the tilted area in front of a player) were easy to follow and grid-based. Bally's "Fireball" (1972) brought a new asymmetrical approach to pinball art and still stands up as a fine example of mechanical era design. Back glass displays are collectible in their own right; older ones from the 1930s to 1960s are particularly appealing. Their

Kiss and make-up

Bally were invited to devise a pinball game for the rock group Kiss in 1978, and the corporation duly obliged with the first ever four-player machine.

The mascara-eyed pomp rockers turned out to be sticklers for accuracy, insisting that on the original stencil drawings the hair length, muscle size, and glam make-up matched theirs identically. A special version of Kiss pinball was produced for the German market, with two rounded s's. It was thought that the original Kiss logo might cause offence.

once crude, trash art aesthetics have, over the years, become charming period pieces.

Generally speaking, digital-era games (post 1978) are more reliable and easier to repair. As when buying a classic sports car, make sure you ask for all the relevant paperwork, including the all-important operating manual, before you part with the cash.

✪ coolest buy Terminator 2

Midway's "Gilligan's Island" may have been the first standard pinball game to have a dot-matrix display, but the awesome T2 was the game everyone wanted to play back in 1991. Dot-matrix thrills aside, this four-player, multi-ball game had enough features to satisfy the most seasoned "pinhead": video game mode, light-up silver skull, gun grip, and swing-out cannon. The playfield is a post-apocalyptic maze of ramps, lane changes, and drop targets. It comes with an Arnie loop that tells you there's an "extra ball".

04 Bally Fireball. 1972.
ⓈⓈⓈⓈ

05 Gorgar. 1979.
ⓈⓈⓈ

✪ Williams Terminator 2 Judgment Day. 1991.
ⓈⓈⓈⓈ

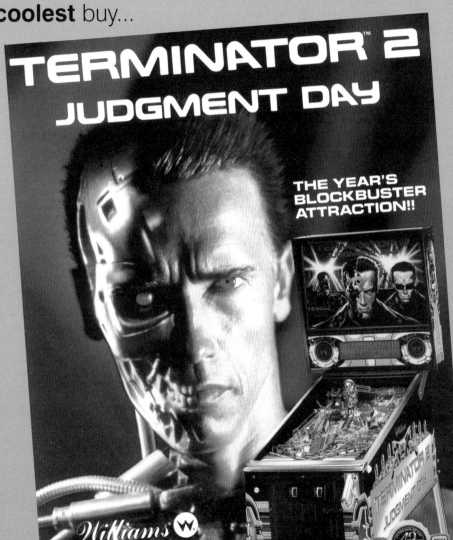

COMPUTER GAMES

Although hard to imagine in these days of online and console gaming with its narrative-style favourites such as Tomb Raider or Quake, the first universally played computer game was a simple game of tennis featuring two straight-line bats and a ball that went "pong".

Officially the first video game was Space War, designed by an IT student in 1962 and played exclusively on the rare and long-obsolete PDP-1 computer. But Pong, the popular home video game by US manufacturers Atari, was the first to hit the high street in the mid 1970s, followed shortly by Coleco's Telstar (dig that mock teak effect!) and the Magnavox Odyssey 4000 in the home consoles market.

By the late 1970s, kids had moved onto arcade games such as Space Invaders and Asteroids and the craze was soon replicated in the home entertainment market by companies like Mattel who brought out their cartridge-loaded Intellivision games console. "A range of programs designed to put a whole new world at your family's fingertips. And right on your own television screen!" as the brochure promised.

The Atari 5200 (with accompanying analogue joystick) and the impressive ColecoVision, armed with cartridges including the popular Donkey Kong, were among the last consoles to be made before video games and their manufacturers suffered a temporary dip in fortunes.

Most deals in vintage computer games are done online, giving these once futuristic-looking plastic and teak-effect offerings a brand new lease of life. Lara Croft beware!

01 Atari Pong. 1976. [$]

02 Magnavox Odyssey 100. 1975. [$]

03 Coleco Telstar. 1977. [$]

04 Mattel Intellivision. 1980. [$]

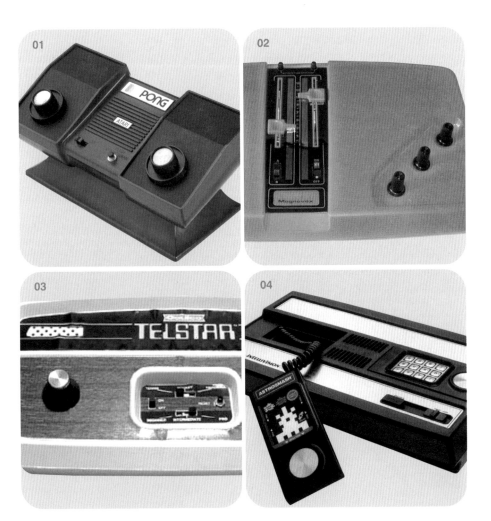

✪ **coolest buy** Space Invaders

The Taito Corporation's 1978 classic in which wave upon wave of alien spacecraft attack players that move horizontally between crumbling dot-matrix defences lays claim to being the most popular arcade game of them all. On its original Japanese launch it was such a success that teenagers stole from their parents and robbed grocery stores for the necessary coins, a state of affairs that prompted a new minting of the yen.

The sets came in both black/white and colour and were manufactured in bar table and stand-up arcade form. A number of later incarnations have also been released including Space Invaders II, Space Invaders De Luxe, and Super Space Invaders '91.

Table-top versions are a better bet as, unlike the larger, cigarette butt-scarred arcade versions, they fit easily into the home. Beware examples that bear no references to either Taito or Midway, their US licensees, as these are likely to be bootleg versions.

05 Atari 5200 (four-port model). 1982. [$]

06 Super Action Controller for ColecoVision. 1982. [$]

✪ **Taito Space Invaders video arcade game. 1978.** [$][$][$][$]

05

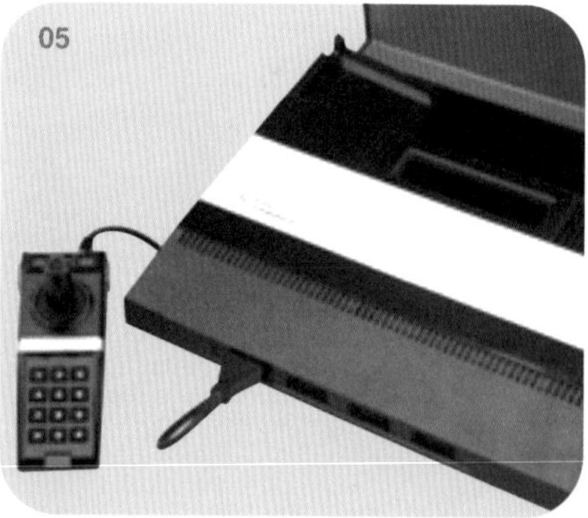

06

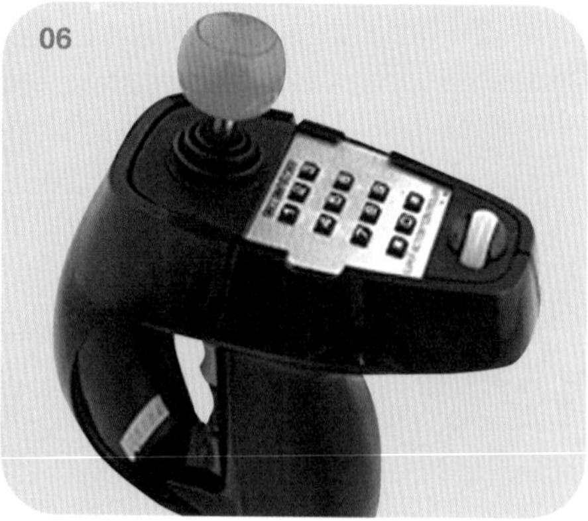

☆ **coolest** buy...

BOARD GAMES

In the days before video and computer games, children and adults alike would while away their evenings with a fold-up board game. Games familiar to the post-war baby boomer such as Monopoly and Cluedo are surprisingly similar to the dice-based race games played in ancient Egypt back in 4000 BC. The Game of Goose, an 18th-century variant, was popular amongst wealthy families in Europe, the French version being a particular favourite of Napoleon's.

Games of the 20th century closely follow their era's interests and fashions, and are excellent social documents as well as being a collectible you can actually enjoy. Some are bought purely for their design or artwork; an old 1930s game of Buccaneer, in which Bakelite pirate ships hunt for buried treasure in the high seas, possesses a quality and finish rarely seen in mass-market objects today.

Thematically, board games can be based around anything from war, the Wild West, or space exploration, yet the most popular game is one in which players go round the board in search of wealth and property. Monopoly, launched in 1935 by US games giant Parker and licensed in the UK by Waddingtons, was originally based on the Atlantic City grid, branching out later to New York, London, and Paris. In the earliest versions, mascots were made in lead alloy while houses and hotels were wooden.

Wartime shortages meant that Monopoly and other popular board games were soon downgraded. Gleaming Scottie dogs, top hats, and boots were replaced with mounted cards, while bone dice gave way to the

Monopoly (UK edition, manufactured by John Waddington Ltd). 1936. $

humble paper spinner. Sets from this era are not as valuable as they might seem, as many will have been worn out by incessant trips around the block. Best wait for a pre-war Monopoly set to turn up.

A sister game Totopoly – "the great race game" – followed soon after, but despite its attractive double-sided board and hollow cast horse and rider figurines, it failed to match the success of Monopoly, which remains a best-seller 70 years after it was first played. Examples of both these vintage Waddingtons games, including the excellent Buccaneer, can still be found in reasonable condition today. Pre-war editions are significantly more valuable than later ones.

Old board games can reveal a lot about the period in which they were devised. Popular 1950s games such as Merit's Magic Robot (in which a diminutive magnetized bot answers a series of general knowledge questions) shows the decade's obsession with sci-fi. Wild West games and games featuring doctors and nurses also proliferated in the post-war era.

02 Totopoly (John Waddington Ltd). 1938. $

03 Buccaneer (John Waddington Ltd). 1938. $$

04 Mastermind (Invicta). $

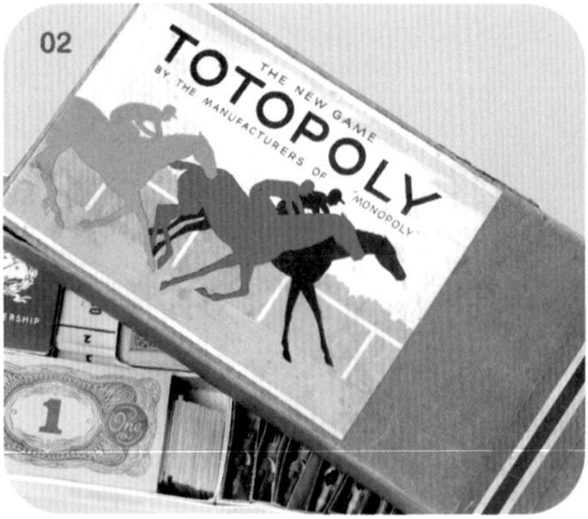

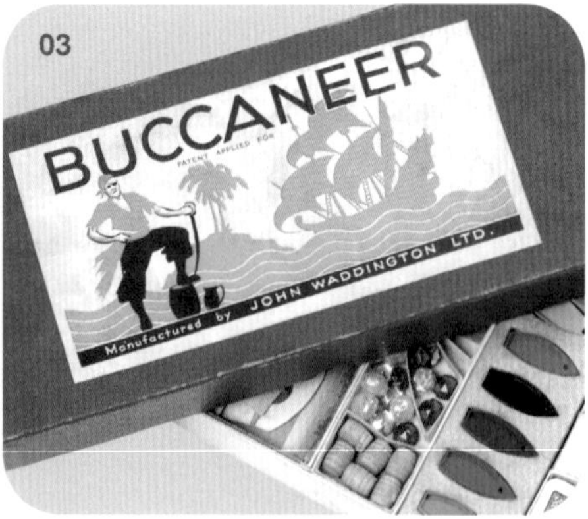

From the 1960s onwards, however, television's increasing hold on the younger generation led to the rise of merchandise-style games like Arrow's Kojak or Palitoy's The Muppet Show. Unlike contemporaries such as the brilliant Mouse Trap Game (made by the Ideal Toy Corporation), the ingenuity or design of the game itself wasn't the deal. These games hit toy shop shelves fast enough to capitalize on their shows' success yet found their way into attics as quickly as their popularity faded.

Board games were ultimately replaced by video and computer games and, sadly, each generation has since found their own form of home entertainment. Who knows whether Counter-Strike or Grand Theft Auto will match Cluedo and Risk in offering future gamers clues to our civilization?

✪ coolest buy War games

Often referred to as strategy games, war games originated in France during the early 1900s. L'Attaque was a simple grid-based affair played

04

Breaking the code

Devised by an Israeli postmaster, and with a box that pictured a bearded playboy-type and an alluring young oriental companion (actually a hairdresser salon owner and a computer science student from the University of Leicester), Master Mind brought "cunning and logic" to the world's living rooms in 1972, with versions going out to at least 33 countries.

with cards mounted on tin bases that represented different ranks in the army. Higher ranking cards such as generals and colonels were able to take cards showing lower ranks.

It proved so popular with warmongering schoolboys that naval and aerial versions were produced (Dover Patrol and Aviation). Tri-Tactics, first made by H.P. Gibson in the 1930s, combined land, sea, and air battles right up until the 1970s, by which time plastic bases had replaced the metal ones.

Another early strategy game, and one that is still played today, is Battleship. Composing originally of simple gridmarked paper and a couple of pencils, Battleship eventually evolved into a set consisting of two plastic trays, some pegs, and several plastic warships. In the 1980s US manufacturer Milton Bradley even brought out an electronic version complete with sound and lights.

During the Cold War era, Risk was the board game that went down best with living-room tacticians. Originally called "La Conquest du Monde" (Conquest of the World), it was co-devised by award-winning film script writer Albert Lamorisse. Parker Brothers bought the rights to the game and released it as the Risk Continental Game in 1959.

By the 1970s World War Two was far enough away to come back into fashion. *The World At War* and *Dad's Army* were never off the television set, and pop stars like Bryan Ferry were dressing like 1940s GIs.

Escape from Colditz, a time-consuming World War Two escape game released on the back of the popular television series starring David MacCallum and Robert Wagner, had superb packaging and included authentic-looking ration books and a history of the real German POW camp. It might have taken hours to get over the fence, but preparing for escape seemed like fun at the time.

72-73 BOARD GAMES

✪ **coolest** buy...

SPACE TOYS

Japan's toy industry produced millions of cheap metal and plastic space toys during the 1950s and 1960s. Today these items are highly collectible and can command serious prices.

Inspired by B-movies, comic strips, and the space race, robots (made by companies like Nomura and Horikawa) were packaged in boxes that bore western-sounding names and spectacular sci-fi art. Their main destination was the US, where science fiction and movies such as *Forbidden Planet* and its TV spin-off *Lost In Space* had taken hold. Robby, its dome-headed star, was much replicated, most effectively by Nomura's Mechanized Robot.

The square-jawed Machine Man, produced in the mid 1950s, is one of the rarest bots on the scene, with boxed versions fetching £30,000 upwards. At the cheaper end of the market are "gear" robots, distinguished by a visible gear mechanism on their chest area. Echoing 1960s pop culture, colour combinations became more daring while details, such as the blinking green eyes on Taiyo's Blink-a-Gear, were a little on the sinister side.

In vintage toy robot world "mint" rarely means perfect. Battery corrosion, chipped paintwork, and missing antennae are the most common complaints, while rust will bring a robot's value down to as little as ten per cent of its mint-condition price.

When George Lucas passed up a $500,000 director's fee for a major cut in *Star Wars* merchandizing and licensing profits, movie insiders must have doubted his sanity. More than 20 years later, however, revenues run well into the billions. Since the release of the first of the *Star Wars* trilogy in 1977,

01 Robby the Robot by Nomura. Tinplate. 1950s. With box: $$$

02 Machine Man by Masudaya. Tin plate, battery operated. 1958. $$$$$

03 Blink-a-Gear by Taiyo. Tin plate, battery-operated. 1950s. $$$

04 Plastic robot. Battery-operated. 1960s. $

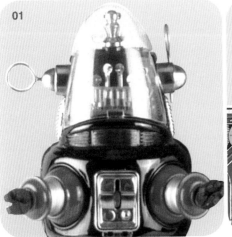

01

02

03

04

spin-off toys were produced all over the world, so there is plenty to choose from – providing the toys remain boxed and undamaged.

✪ **coolest buy** Ray guns

Buck Rogers, the all-American guy who wakes up to find himself in the 25th century, was the inspiration for the first toy ray gun, made of cardboard and used as a promotional gimmick for Cocomalt cereal in 1933.

Earthly children would have been far happier with later models, made of die cast, pressed metal, or aluminium. Throughout the 1950s and 1960s it was the Japanese who produced the galaxy's best tin space pistols and rifles, notably Nomura's Space Control Gun and Daiya's Super Sonic Gun.

With baroque chrome-effect casting, Hubley's Atomic Disintegrator remains one of the most sought after US-made guns. UK toy makers also produced their fair share of interstellar weaponry; Lone Star's Dan Dare Cap Gun, inspired by the space traveller from *The Eagle*, was much imitated.

05 Darth Vader and C3PO *Star Wars* figures. 1977. $

06 All Terrain Armoured Transport, from *The Empire Strikes Back*. 1981. $$

✪ 1950s and 60s ray guns from the US, Japan, and UK. $$–$$$

05

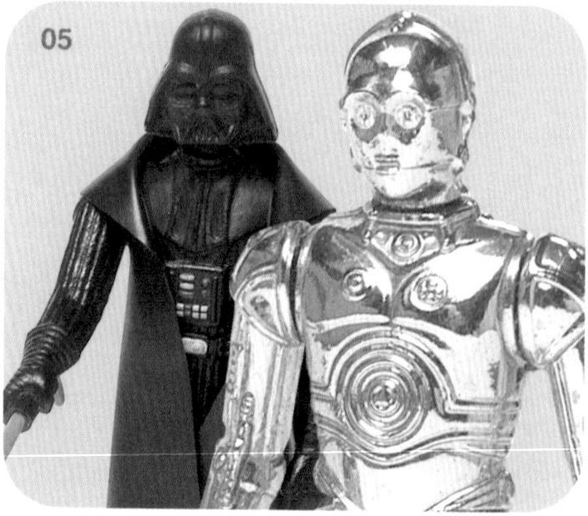

06

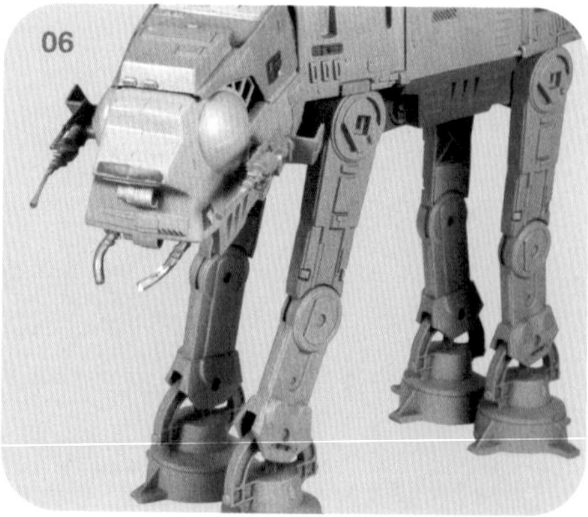

SPACE CONTROL

DAN DARE

ROCKET GUN
SAFETY MODE

2 SAFETY ROCKETS
WITH SECRET
MESSAGE CHAMBER

ATOMIC
DISINTEGRATOR

ATOMIC 200 300 400 500
DISINTEGRATOR

ATOMIC
DISINTEGRATOR

REPEATING
CAP PISTOL
by
HUBLEY

TOY CARS

Although their motoring manufacturers were no match for the mighty Ford, Chrysler, and General Motors, the British led the field in die-cast miniature replica cars from the 1930s up until the late 1960s.

Tin-plate toys were popular amongst well-heeled Victorian children, but at the beginning of the 20th century these gave way to lead and zinc die-cast versions, which proved less harmful to their young owners. Dinky, which evolved from Meccano's "Model Miniatures" range, produced a steady supply of delivery vans and racing cars during the 1930s, but the war halted production, as the nation's tin toys were sacrificed for the military's needs.

Post-war Dinky vehicles appeared with fatter wheels and black base plates, but their market share was soon taken over by a couple of ex-naval servicemen who named their company Matchbox. Offering smaller, neatly boxed die-cast models that were sold through small high street retailers, Matchbox quickly got ahead of Dinky. The Matchbox dark green Morris Minor was a particular favourite, as were their fire engines, tractors, and double-decker buses.

A third toy manufacturer to enter the toy car race was Corgi. The Swansea-based firm had been around since the 1930s, trading under the name Mettoy, but as Corgi they introduced the first die-cast miniature cars with clear windows. Later innovations included bonnets that revealed gleaming engines, boots with spare tyres, and "Glidamatic" suspension, which allowed them to be whizzed along kitchen floors more smoothly than their competitors.

Dinky Packard Clipper Sedan. 1950s. Ⓢ

DINKY TOYS

PACKARD CLIPP

The Batmobile, made by Corgi from 1966 to 1977, was a commercial tie-in with the popular *Batman* television series starring Adam West and Burt Ward. Modelled on custom car king George Barris's version of a Lincoln Futura, the toy was equipped with rocket launcher and front-mounted slasher blade: "Five inches of danger!" as the US ad campaign put it. About five million were sold around the world, collectors paying up to £400 ($640) for existing models today.

Other 1960s Corgis worth looking out for are the *The Man From U.N.C.L.E.* Oldsmobile, produced in dark blue and a rarer white, and the Green Hornet's Black Beauty from the cult US television series starring kung fu legend Bruce Lee.

As pop music broke social and generational barriers, Corgi responded with the Monkeemobile, a 4½-inch replica of the Pontiac GTO hot rod that appeared in *The Monkees* television series. In 1969, before a fire was to devastate their Swansea warehouse, Corgi brought out their miniaturized

02 Matchbox Kingsize Foden dumper truck. c.1960. $

03 Matchbox Moco No. 1 Steam roller. Early 1950s. $

04 Corgi Oldsmobile Tornado. 1960s. $

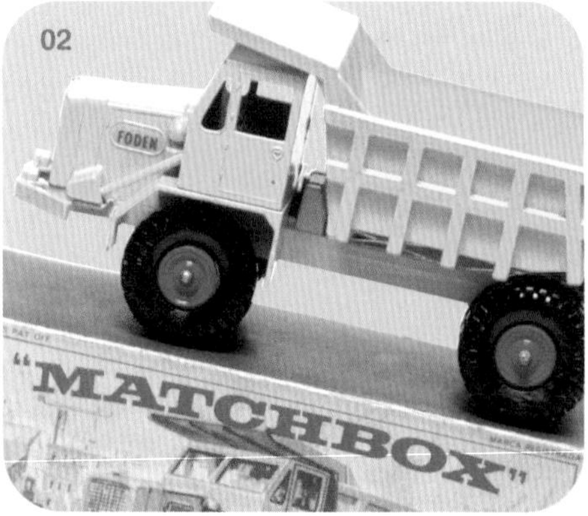

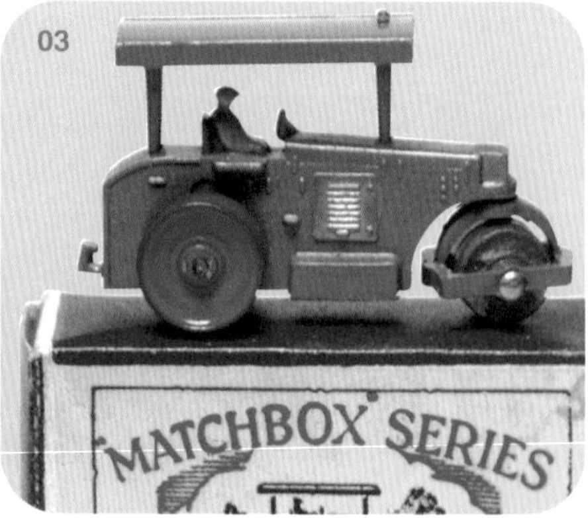

version of The Beatles Yellow Submarine. As in the feature-length animated cartoon, it had rotating periscopes and hatches from which figurines of the Fab Four emerged. On 1960s models (it was also reissued as a Corgi Classic in the late 1990s) white and yellow hatches are rarer than red ones. Collectors pay over £1,000 ($1,600) for mint examples.

The British toy car boom lasted until the early 1970s, when cheaper rivals from China and the Far East came onto the market. Dinkier arrivals from the US such as Mattel's "Hot Wheels" also helped hasten the decline of the UK's die-cast toy industry.

Today Corgi produce limited-edition reissues aimed purely at collectors, but the models originally aimed at impressionable young baby boomers are harder to find in good condition. Avoid repainted cars and make sure they come in their original box, which must itself be undamaged. Values are cut drastically when boxes are torn or crushed. Serious collectors keep their vehicles in airtight containers and away from direct sunlight.

✪ coolest buy Aston Martin DB5

The 1960s was an exciting decade in terms of cars, fashion, and popular entertainment, so it is hardly surprising that Corgi's best-loved models hail from the period.

James Bond's Aston Martin DB5, first previewed in the film *Dr No*, reached the toy shops in 1965. Bond had previously driven a Bentley, but the DB5 was the first Bond car to be modified and armed with an array of baddy-beating custom details.

The replica was no different, and featured front-mounted guns, rear bullet shield, and best of all a working ejector seat. Models were produced in silver and gold plate, and nearly 4 million of them were sold worldwide.

Gold-plated versions are rarer and command prices of up to £1,000 ($1600) today if in mint condition and boxed. Not bad for a toy that sold for the equivalent of a few weeks' pocket money in its day.

05 Corgi Yellow Submarine. 1969. $$

06 Corgi Man from U.N.C.L.E. Thrush-buster. 1966. $$

✪ Corgi James Bond Aston Martin DB5. 1965–9. $$

05

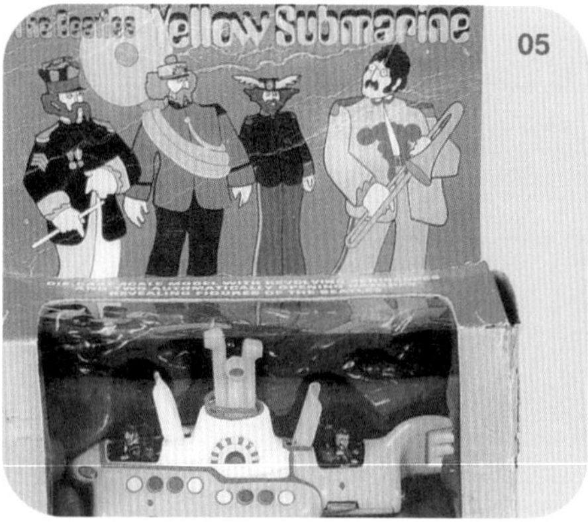

06

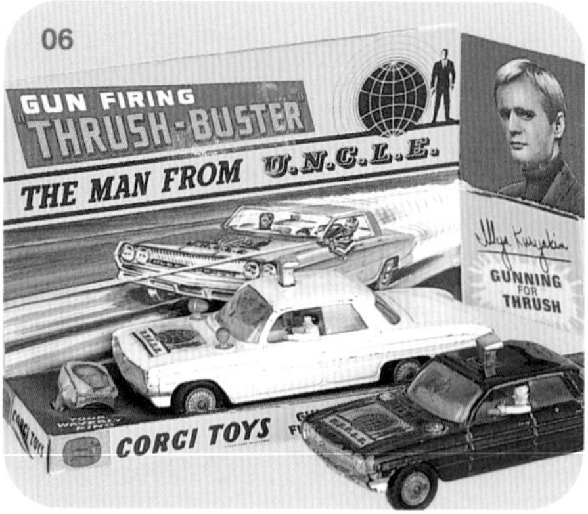

CAMERAS

--->

Although the first photograph was thought to have been taken as long ago as the 1820s, it wasn't until the turn of the century that photography became a hobby that everyone could indulge in. "You press the button, we do the rest" ran the slogan to Kodak's Brownie box camera, launched in 1900.

With their strong technical savvy and an existing optical industry, Germany headed the production of handy-sized 35mm cameras right up until the 1960s.

Zeiss of Dresden, renowned for their Contax and Kolibri models, produced the Super Ikonta B from the early 1930s to the mid 1950s. A good-looking, large negative camera that folds completely flat, it will still take a great picture today – providing you can find the accompanying 120mm roll film.

Made from 1954 to 1966 by German manufacturers Leitz, the Leica M3 featured the innovative bayonet-mounted lens and lever wind film advance. Its unequalled robustness and quality of build immediately found favour with Henri Cartier-Bresson, Robert Doisneau, and other early Magnum photo-journalists. Only 250,000 were madem of which the first batch are most collectible. Look out for serial numbers 700,000–700,800 (made in 1954).

Victor Hasselblad developed single lens reflex (SLR) cameras for the Swedish military in the 1940s. After playing an important role in early aerial photography, the eponymous Hasselblad went on to become a profes-sional's favourite, even taking some of the first pictures of the moon during the 1969 Apollo 11 mission. Up to 12 Hasselblad cameras are believed to

Zeiss Ikon Super Ikonta B. 1950. Ⓢ Ⓢ

have been left on the lunar surface, their films having been brought down to earth.

For 1960s "Swinging London" fashion photographers such as Terence Donavan and David Bailey (Bailey's first camera was a Rollei 6 x 6), the Rolleiflex 2.8 was the ultimate studio accessory. The makers of this now classic twin lens reflex camera had a long-lasting gentleman's agreement with SLR-specialists Hasselblad not to simultaneously release competing cameras. The compact Rollei 35, launched in 1970, is another cult favourite, with versions made in platinum and gold.

Japanese cameras like the classic Nikon F began to flood the market in the early 1960s, spelling an end to German domination. The Nikon F helped define the shape of the modern-day SLR camera and showed the world that the Japanese could come up with a quality piece of kit.

Being used by man-about-town snapper David Hemmings in the 1966 film *Blow Up* didn't do sales any harm, but it also became a favourite amongst

02 Leica M3. 1959. $$$

03 Polaroid 1000 Land Camera. Late 1970s. $

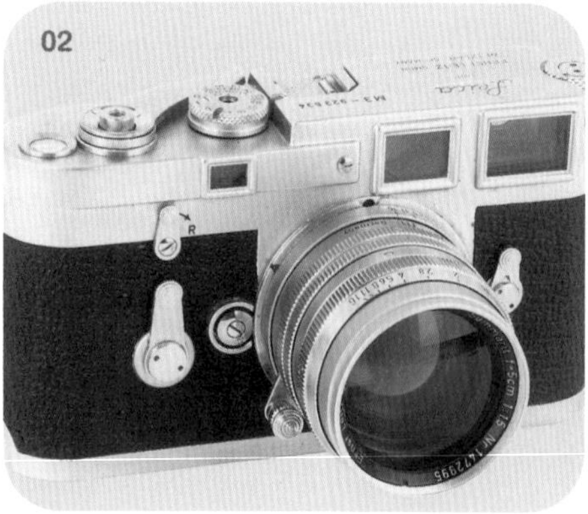

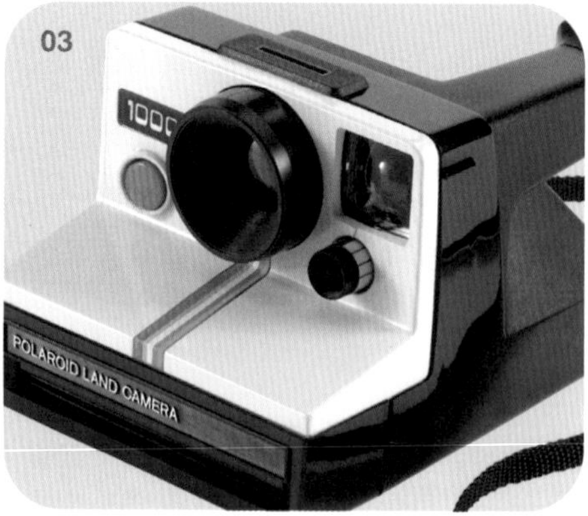

new colour supplement photojournalists like Don McCullin, who was saved from a stray bullet by this sturdy performer while on assignment in Cambodia. The Nikon F is as timeless as a Porsche or a Savile Row suit, and even today its lens remains compatible with much later Nikon models.

Today's top-of-the range digital successors may have the technological edge over cameras of the past, but classic cameras remain very much in use and can be easily maintained or repaired. Enthusiasts focus their collections around themes such as era, camera type, or manufacturer. Interesting or unusual working mechanisms always attract interest. Leica is the hottest name of all, although 1960s and 1970s Nikon, Canon, and Pentax are beginning to command high prices.

Like any professional equipment, cameras that turn up on the second-hand market should be generally well looked after, but don't buy if body condition is poor (scratched leather, surface dents, etc) or shutter and focusing mechanism are damaged.

An instant cult

Polaroid is a byword for instant photography and this early 1970s model from Edwin Land's US-based company had a neat folding design and could fit inside a suit pocket.

The SX-70 quickly found favour with artists and designers – among them Andy Warhol and Charles Eames – who saw the creative possibilities of manipulating the light-sensitive Polaroid paper. SX-70s can be picked up relatively cheaply today, although you'll have a harder job tracking down the original Polaroid flash mounts.

✪ **coolest buy** Minox spy camera

Also known as sub-miniatures, spy cameras are even smaller than the once miniature 35mm format. The best and most original is the Minox, invented by a Latvian called Walter Zapp.

With ambitions to manufacture a camera that was shorter than a cigar and less heavy than a cigarette lighter, Zapp came up with the Ur-Minox in 1938. Amazingly, it took 8 x 11mm film and could be hidden in the palm of the user's hand.

His cameras became favourites with real-life and fictional spies, among them James Bond and Harry Palmer. The 1969 Minox B with its excellent lens and built-in exposure is the quintessential Cold War spy camera. Minox cameras are still produced today and are made by Leica in Germany.

Other classic sub-miniatures to look out for include Rollei 16s, Minolta 16s, and the Swiss-made Tessina, a twin lens reflex camera that is actually *smaller* than a pack of cigarettes.

04 Hassleblad 500C/M. 1972. Ⓢ Ⓢ Ⓢ

05 Nikon F. 1962. Ⓢ Ⓢ

✪ Minox B and flash gun with box. 1969. Ⓢ Ⓢ

✪ coolest buy...

STYLE STYLE STYLE ST

STYLE STYLE

YLE STYLE ST

STYLE STYLE

STYLE STYLE STYLE STYLE

STYLE STYLE

INTRODUCTION

Fashion is always looking backwards for inspiration, and original vintage clothing is an affordable and practical alternative to the often inferior items trotted out by today's designers.

From 1940s Hawaiian shirts to bomber jackets and blue jeans, America has the biggest influence on retro cool. James Dean and the Vietnam War may be a distant memory, but their sartorial influence still looms large in the collector's closet.

While America gave us denim and the T-shirt, the sneaker is a more global phenomenon. Old or never-been-sold Air Maxes and Gazelles are today finding a new kind of buyer, the sneaker freak. Unlikely ever to actually wear these street-smart classics, these chroniclers of cool are always on the lookout for the rarest colourways or limited-edition releases from Nike, Adidas, Puma, and the rest.

Collecting retro style almost inevitably leads to an Aladdin's cave of fashion accessories: watches worn by Le Mans racing drivers or Soviet space pioneers, sunglasses that once perched on the noses of F-16 fighter pilots, or ties that hung from the necks of Be-Bop trumpeters. Something, in fact, for everyone to blow their horn about.

HAWAIIAN SHIRTS

By the time mass tourism found this South Sea island paradise, the Aloha shirt was already a popular line in the Hawaiian garment trade.

Produced in an infinite number of styles and designs, and famously worn by Elvis Presley and Presidents Harry Truman and Dwight Eisenhower, the classic Hawaiian shirt remains an individual and highly flamboyant item of casual clothing. It is also valued highly for its beauty and connection to these tropical islands famous for surfing and exotic flora.

Collectors regard the 1940s and 1950s as the "golden age" of Hawaiian shirts. Mostly made of synthetic rayon and depicting typical local scenes (coconut groves, pineapples, hibiscus flowers, etc), they should carry the "Made In Hawaii" labels of makers such as Shaheen and Musa-Shiya.

The "Made in Hawaii" tag was an indication that the buyer was getting a quality home-spun garment and arguably more authentic than ones which were later mass produced in America and Japan. Buttons on these earlier versions were made mostly from hand-polished coconut which complements the exotic fabric patterns beautifully.

When rayon declined in the 1950s, cotton variations appeared more regularly. Although much less valuable than their enduring rayon predecessors, they are becoming increasingly rated by dealers and buyers alike. Look for bold floral prints from the Surf Line label and Reyn Spooner, pioneers of the reverse-print shirt.

These feel-good items of clothing didn't only reflect the best of Hawaii; many from the classic rayon era depict popular Japanese symbols like

01 Niagra Falls print. Rayon. 1960s. [$]

02 Lemon Lilly print. Cotton. 1960s. [$]

03 Welcome to Hawaii print. Cotton. 1960s. [$][$]

04 Coral print. Cotton. 1960s. [$]

tigers or Mount Fuji. Border shirts, on which the design covers the whole garment, command higher prices, and long-sleeved rayon Hawaiian shirts can be worth up to twice the amount of a short-sleeved version.

Before buying a vintage Aloha shirt, check that the fabric and buttons are undamaged; also make sure that the breast pocket matches the rest of the shirt. Wear it large and wear it proud.

✪ **coolest buy** "The Montgomery Clift"

In the 1954 film *From Here to Eternity*, set around a military base on Hawaii in the run up to Pearl Harbor, actor Montgomery Clift can be seen in at least three types of Aloha shirt. The most famous is the black border shirt depicting Hawaii's Diamond Head mountain that Clift wears before dying on the golf course. This Duke Kahanamoku design, featuring native Hawaiian leaves, also appears in the film, in the scene where Clift kills Ernest Borgnine.

05 Brown and orange print. Cotton. Late 1950s. [$][$]

06 Long-sleeved pineapple print. Rayon. Late 1940s/early 1950s. [$][$][$]

✪ Duke Kahanamoku Hawaiian leaf print. Rayon. 1936–43. [$][$]

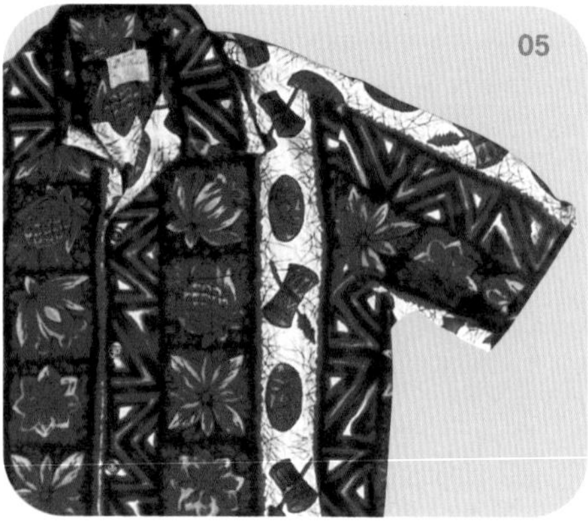

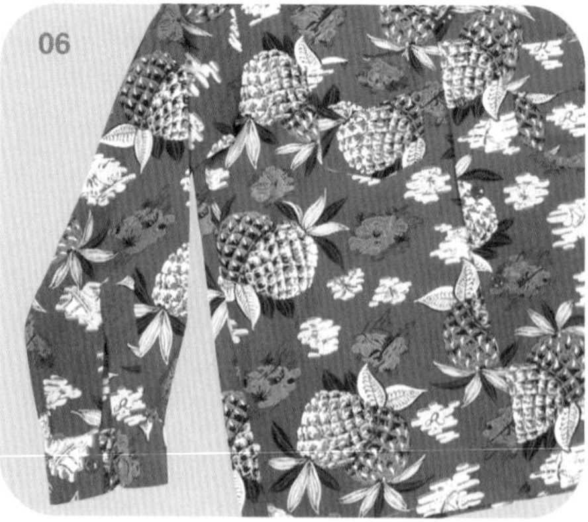

★ **coolest** buy...

DENIM

When Marlon Brando wore them in *The Wild One*, jeans reached near-iconic status, yet during the 19th century denim was used primarily for manufacturing work overalls, and for years this hard-wearing and comfortable material remained a humble staple for the American blue collar worker.

Levi's, the San Francisco-based company started in 1853 by Bavarian immigrant Levi Strauss, introduced the now ubiquitous copper rivets. The earliest pairs had cinch buckle backs instead of belt loops and were known as "waist overalls" until the 1950s when teenagers began to call them jeans. The legendary 501 didn't appear until the 1940s. Early versions (marked Lot 501 XX) sported paper "Two Horse" patches; later ones have them in leather.

Look out for Levi's with a big "E" on the famous red pocket logo. This, along with a stitched V shape next to the top fly button, indicates that the jean will have been made before 1971. Another tell-tale sign are two red lines which run along the inside white selvage material. This shows that they are pre-1985 vintage and therefore highly collectible.

Ohio-based H.D. Lee company made their name with the popular bib overall, as worn by Depression-era sharecroppers. Although they didn't manufacture jeans until the 1940s, Lee pioneered the use of the zipper to replace the button fly and clothed real-life cowboys and US servicemen.

Wrangler, formerly called the Blue Bell Overall Company (pre-1970s items also carry the Blue Bell logo), produced a range of denim jeans and jackets which were tried and tested by professional rodeo riders. With visible seams and boot-cut leg, the Wrangler "Cowboy Cut" jean was launched in 1947.

Levi's 501 XX. 1950s.
$ $

Vintage denim attracts vast sums of money today, and dealers have practically exhausted markets in Europe, USA, and Japan. Serious denim collectors head for the American Mid-West, where they hope to unearth supplies of 80-year-old work smocks in someone's barn. With a little knowledge of rivets, grading, and labels, who knows when they might strike gold?

✪ **coolest buy** Denim jackets

Worn by ranchers, rebels, and rockers, the denim jacket has been reinvented many times over the years.

Levi's have been making denim jackets since the 1920s. "Firsts" (or the 506 XX) had a single front pocket and rear black buckle clasp, while "seconds" (507 XX) sported silver buttons, twin pockets, and front pleats.

Lee jackets go back to the 1930s, the most wearable being the twin-pocketed 101J. The sewn-in collar label usually offers the best guide to age, for example pre-1969 Lee labels omit the words "Union Made".

02 Detail of the Levi's big "E" pocket tab indicating pre-1971 jeans.

03 Detail of early Levi's "cinch back" jeans.

✪ Three vintage denim jackets – Lee 101J, Levi's 507 XX, and Blue Bell Wrangler 8MJL. 1950s to early 1960s. Ⓢ Ⓢ

100-101 DENIM

T-SHIRTS

Up until the 1950s, the T-shirt had really only been worn by off-duty World War Two servicemen and high school jocks. After James Dean's performance in *Rebel Without a Cause*, however, this cotton undergarment became a potent symbol of youth rebellion.

Initially, these cheap throwaway items of clothing were seen as an effective way of promotion. The earliest example of this was a shirt advertising the launch of the film *The Wizard of Oz* in 1939, while Jean Seberg's New York *Herald Tribune* shirt, seen in the Jean-Luc Godard film *A Bout de Souffle*, briefly became a hip item in the late 1950s.

Virtually every brand has put their name on a T; the old white-on-red Coca-Cola shirt was recently voted "the most iconic T-shirt of all time". Other favoured branded T's include the Nike swoosh, the three-striped 1970s Adidas, and hard-as-nails boxing staple, the Lonsdale.

While Californian hot rod car culture peaked in the early 1960s, custom car artist and designer Ed "Big Daddy" Roth made a tidy living by selling custom airbrushed T-shirts at car shows. His shirts depicting monsters driving far-out hot rods became so popular that he ended up buying a silk-screen machine. His most famous creation was vile road rodent, the Rat Fink.

Down the years, fashion designers have created their own versions of the T-shirt, including Paul Smith, Karl Lagerfield, and Katherine Hamnett. The latter famously donned her black on white "74% Don't Want Pershing" shirt to meet Prime Minister Thatcher, kick-starting the short-lived 1984 trend that gave us "Choose Life" and "Frankie Say Arm The Unemployed".

01 Adidas T-shirt. 1980s. $

Former Kings Road punk couturier Vivienne Westwood was responsible for the long-sleeved "Naked Cowboys" and "Chaos" T-shirts sold from her and partner Malcolm McLaren's Seditionaries boutique in the late 1970s. All are highly collectible today and go for four-figure sums at auction.

Westwood items excepted, T-shirts are one of the few garments that definitely look better with age. It doesn't have to be summer to wear a vintage T. Choose softer cottons with washed out, chipped, or faded logos.

✪ **coolest buy** Rock T-shirts

The rock tour T-shirt with iron-on band logo is the ultimate sign of fan loyalty. With second-hand band T-shirts your affiliation is hardly a matter of life and death, although it does help if it's a group that currently has kudos or influence. Of the vintage band T-shirts, Run DMC, and AC/DC are the most popular among the cognoscenti, although there have been sightings of Kraftwerk, Iron Maiden, and even Mancunian indie legend Joy Division.

02 Lonsdale T-shirt. 1980s. [$]

03 Rat Fink T-shirt by Ed Roth. 1985. [$]

✪ Rock T-shirts. White sleeveless Iron Maiden (late 1980s). Black Iron Maiden (1992). Motörhead (early 1980s). [$]

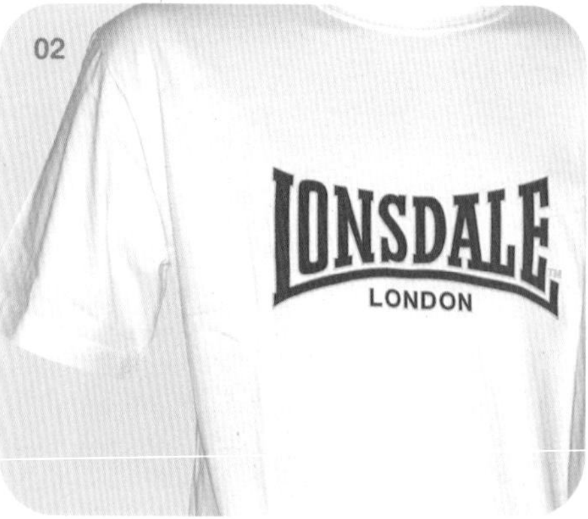

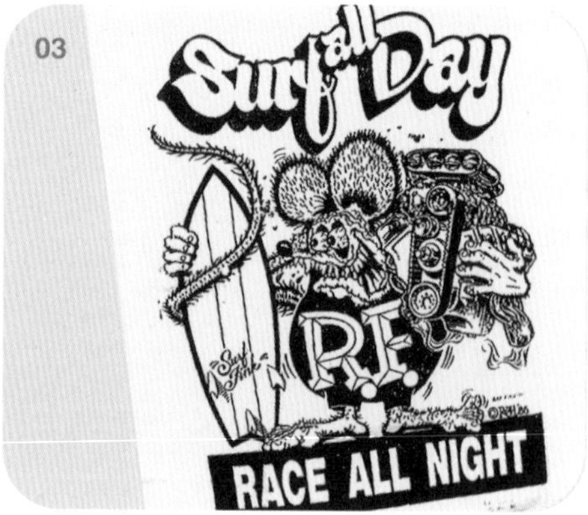

✪ **coolest** buy...

SNEAKERS

The sports sneaker has become the defining item of clothing for a generation. Sneakers are big business today, with customers looking to buy new designs on almost a weekly basis.

The market for used sneakers or dead stock (boxed items that never actually changed hands) is no different, except that buyers have a much better understanding of the shoe. They know not only who made them and when, but who designed them and all the colour combinations they came in. With leading manufacturers like Nike and Adidas bringing out reissues, sneaker freaks need to be as fast on their toes as the athletes who promote them.

Nike shoes attract the largest number of devotees. The company started by Phil Knight and Bill Bowerman retains the utmost respect from the street, while stars such as Tiger Woods and Michael Jordan embody the Nike attitude in the sports arena.

Former runner Knight was responsible for inventing the waffle-soled sneaker back in 1972 after pouring some rubber into a kitchen waffle iron. The Air Force One basketball boot was conceived ten years later, followed shortly after by the near mythical Air Jordan. Another collector's favourite, the Air Max, first came out in 1995. Designed by Nike vice president Tinker Hatfield, they were the first trainer to be equipped with an air bubble.

Adidas, the long-running German company started by Adi Dassler, made the shoes worn by Jesse Owens in the 1936 Olympics. The famous three stripes first appeared in 1949, while the Adidas trefoil symbol, found usually on the shoe's tongue, wasn't used until 1972.

Nike Waffle II. Deadstock with original box. 1979.
$ $

Adidas collectors prefer "old skool" designs like the Run DMC-endorsed Superstar, although the 1984 Micro Pacer has undoubted cachet for its silver leather finish and in-built microprocessor. Dassler's brother Rudi launched his rival Puma brand in 1948 and the distinctive shoes have been showcased by Pele and The Beastie Boys.

When tracking old trainers, check the original date of issue, usually indicated by the first two digits printed on the serial number inside. Serious collectors insist they come unworn in their original box and preferably still wrapped in virgin tissue paper. Only sizes above UK six are considered.

✪ **coolest buy** Air Jordan 1s

Michael Jordan's white, red, and black Air Jordan 1s fell foul of NBA rules when they came out in 1985. Black shoes weren't allowed on pro courts and Nike's rising star was fined $1,000 (£600) every time he put them on. At least 17 colour combos were later released, including a very rare black and grey.

02 Record by Adidas. Early 1980s. $

03 Canada by Puma. Early 1980s. $

✪ Air Jordan 1 by Nike. 1985. Deadstock with original box: $$$$

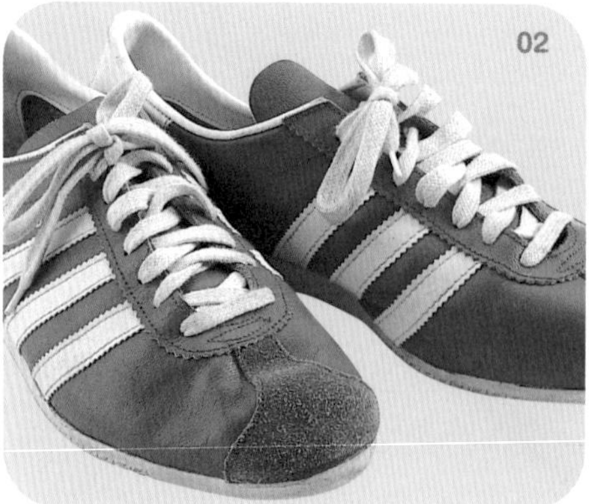

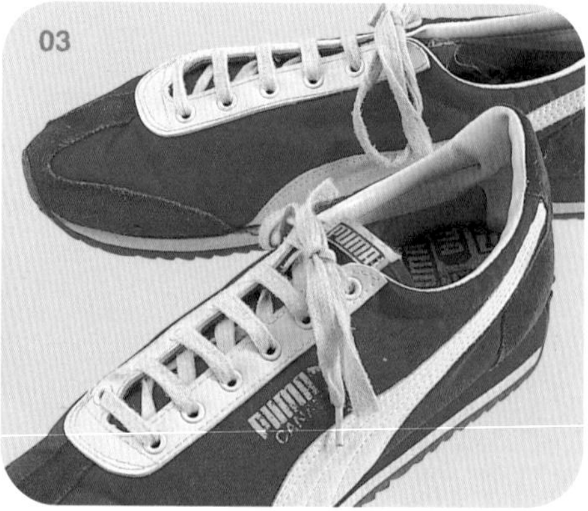

✪ **coolest** buy...

WATCHES

-->

Part gadget, part fashion accessory, and an essential piece of kit for pilots, divers, adventurers, and racing drivers, the wristwatch is the ideal collectible object. Twentieth-century watches are relatively easy to find and maintain. They are also items that gain in value whilst being shown off daily.

The earliest wristwatches appeared in the early 1900s and quickly replaced the fob watch which was pocketed via a chain in a jacket. Hands-free watches particularly appealed to early aviation pioneers, and one, Alberto Santos-Dumont, had one made for him by his friend Henri Cartier after a conversation they had in Maxim's Paris nightclub. The high-flying Brazilian used it to check his record-breaking 220-metre flight, which took just 21 seconds in November 1907.

Swiss manufacturers Omega supplied British World War One fighter pilots with wrist chronographs (watches with at least two independent time systems). Their 1969 Flightmaster was the last to be made specifically for aeroplane pilots. With colour-coded winders and distinctive red and blue hands, this sky-bound heavyweight has a jet engraved on its back. There are believed to be around 40 gold versions in existence, all of which would fetch thousands today.

Around the same time, another jaw-dropping Omega, the Speedmaster, was being launched into space by US astronauts. To help NASA reach a decision about which watch their space personnel should be issued with, a number of competing products underwent rigorous laboratory tests, including boiling at 93 degrees and freezing at 18 below zero. The

01 Omega
Speedmaster 125.
1973. Ⓢ Ⓢ Ⓢ Ⓢ

02 Eterna KonTiki.
2003. Ⓢ Ⓢ Ⓢ Ⓢ

03 Tag Heuer Monaco
Steve McQueen. 1970s.
Ⓢ Ⓢ Ⓢ Ⓢ

04 Tag Heuer Jacky Ickx
Easy Rider. c.1970.
Ⓢ Ⓢ Ⓢ

victorious Speedmaster was worn by Apollo 11 astronauts when they landed on the moon at 02:56 GMT on 21 July 1969. For this reason, it is popularly known as the "moon watch".

Rolex claimed to be the first manufacturer to build a hermetically sealed water resistant watch. Named the Oyster, it was soon put to the test by Mercedes Gleitze, a young swimmer who wore it to cross the English Channel in 1927, an event which gave their new product priceless publicity. The luxury watch makers went on to make the first submariner's diving watch (the Sea Dweller), the first day/date display model (the President), and the time zone-busting GMT Master.

One of the most curious and valuable diver's watches is the Omega Seamaster 600 "ploprof" (plongeur professional). Featuring deep sea rubber strap and button press, and bi-directional diver's bezel, this 1970 model found favour with French marine biologist Jacques Cousteau, who tested it on Operation Janus, his 500-metre deep exploration off the coast of Corsica.

05 Scuba Swatch by Vivienne Westwood. 1990. [$][$]

06 Hamilton Pulsar Calculator Watch. 1973. [$][$]

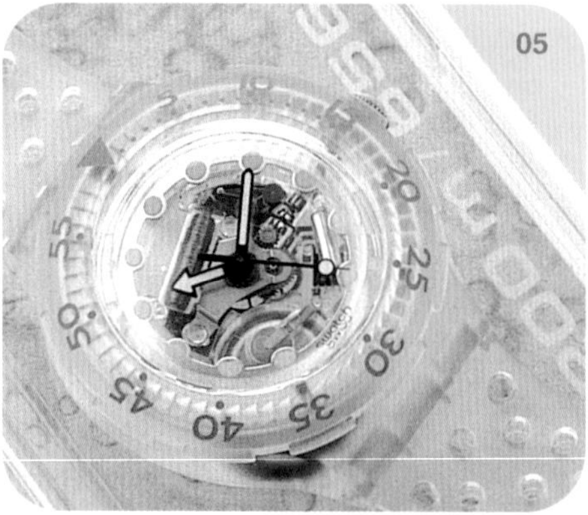

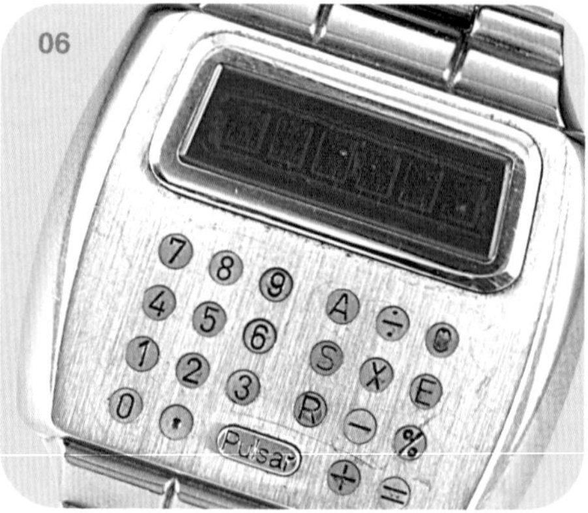

Another explorer to be linked to a classic wristwatch is the Norwegian Thor Heyerdhal. The famous voyage on his KonTiki raft was commemorated by Swiss watch manufacturers Eterna. Although hard to find, these 1950s adventure watches are a good buy compared to similar pieces made by better-known makers.

Heuer, or TAG Heuer as they are known today, have had a long-lasting connection with motor racing. They developed the first dashboard stopwatch for professional racing drivers and launched the Carrera, the first racing chronograph, in the mid 1960s.

Updating the racing watch in 1969, Heuer brought out the Monaco. Worn by Steve McQueen in the film *Le Mans*, it was squarer in design and had a metallic blue face with red and orange chronograph dials protected by a thick layer of Plexiglas. The Monaco has since been relaunched by TAG Heuer, but the original, with punch hole racing strap and left-side winder, remains one of the most wanted time pieces around.

Cheap, cheerful... collectible

Clad in low-cost plastic and inspired by the fashion industry with its constant demand for new collections, Swatch was launched in 1982. Initial designs were in plain colours, although a transparent Swatch was released to show off its 51 working parts (as opposed to the 90 or so in other watches). Swatch also commissioned Vivienne Westwood and New York graffiti artist Keith Haring to come up with designs. These 1980s designer watches are surprisingly valuable today.

Heuer made another classic 1970s racing watch, the Jacky Ickx "Easy Rider". Ickx was a Belgian driver who claimed a record six victories in the gruelling 24-hour Le Mans circuit. The eponymous signed chronograph (also released by Sorna) features 17 jewels and a multi-coloured face.

Quartz crystal LED display watches began to appear in the 1970s. The earliest versions, such as the Pulsar "Time Computer", needed 4.5 volt batteries that had to be recharged every six months. Roger Moore sported something similar in the Bond film *Live And Let Die*.

By the mid 1970s, makers such as Texas Instruments and Citizen were producing more affordable versions, and competing manufacturers made repeated attempts at technical one-upmanship; witness Orient's "Touchtron" with touch-sensitive LED display on Pulsar's chunky six-digit "Calculator Watch" that came with its very own pen/stylus.

With high production levels of LEDs (and the less power hungry LCDs) there are a lot of makes to choose from. Many of the names reflect the overtly futuristic quality of the product. Zytronic, Jupiter, and Uranus may not have lasted, but they remain a fun, eye-catching relic from a more visionary age.

When buying any vintage watch check that it's in good working order. Damaged lugs or defective winding mechanisms can lead to costly repairs.

✪ Omega Olympic Watch. 1973. $$$

✪ **coolest buy** Omega Olympic Watch

Commemorating the 1976 Montreal Olympics, this rare and exciting watch takes its inspiration from the giant stadium scoreboard. Watch buffs may recognize this chunky 1970s timepiece as an old chrono-quartz Omega Seamaster, but that's where the similarity ends. The impressive wrist scoreboard boasts analogue and LED functions, including lap and split-second timer. A must for athletes and retro technophiles alike.

SUNGLASSES

Although Eskimos wore crude sun protectors and dark lenses have long been in use for the treatment of eye problems, sunglasses didn't become fashionable until the 1930s. Back then, frames were made from metal or thick tortoiseshell plastic and lenses were made from heavy glass.

Sunglasses were (and are) an essential glamour accessory, then worn almost exclusively by film stars and the few that could afford foreign travel. Ray-Ban by Bausch and Lomb (est 1937) brought out the Aviator in the 1950s, licensing it to a number of companies including ballistic eyewear manufacturers Randolph Engineering. Randolph was supplying the Aviator to the US Air Force long before Tom Cruise donned a pair in the film *Top Gun*. The metal Aviator has been reinvented by eyewear manufacturers all over the world, but the original Ray-Bans (as favoured by writer Hunter S. Thompson and Robert De Niro in *Taxi Driver*) are the ones to have.

As modelled by James Dean and The Velvet Underground, the other classic Ray-Ban design is the Wayfarer. Streamline chunky plastic frames and thick dark lenses appealed to the 1960s sunglasses-after-dark crowd and continue to influence the style of sunglasses today.

Edwin Land and his company Polaroid pioneered the polarizing sun filter back in the late 1920s. Along with Reactolite Rapide lenses, Polaroid are now associated with the plastic aviator look popular in the 1970s, but thanks to stars like Jarvis Cocker this once unfashionable style is starting to attract reasonable prices. Silver metal-framed Polaroids (think late Elvis) are particularly desirable yet can be snapped up for as little as £20.

01 Ray-Ban Aviator by Bausch and Lomb. Late 1940s. ⓢⓢ

02 Cutler and Gross Model 692. ⓢⓢ

03 Cutler and Gross Model 279. ⓢⓢ

04 Ray-Ban Wayfarer by Bausch and Lomb. Late 1950s/early 1960s. ⓢ

London-based Cutler and Gross specialize in designer sunglasses based on classic frame shapes. Most wanted designs are black plastic wraparounds (as worn by Bono and Lenny Kravitz) and the Cold War spy look as seen in the Michael Caine film *The Ipcress File*.

✪ **coolest buy** Cazal

Originally designed for jet-setting dowagers, this brand of German eyewear became a must-have item for the 1980s hip hop crowd. So much so that in March 1984 the *Philadelphia Times* asked, "Why are kids being killed for these glasses?"

Surely the answer was obvious. With coloured lenses, outrageous gold-plated detail, and a highly visible graffiti-style logo, they were like nothing else on the block. Cazals had numbers, not names, and sounded like they belonged on a Porsche. Famous Cazal wearers have been Run DMC (sporting the now rereleased 607 model) and Al Pacino in *Donnie Brasco*.

05 Tom Cruise sports Ray-Ban Aviators in *Top Gun* (1986).

06 Polaroid 6102 Rally. c.1970. $

✪ Cazal Model 607. 1980s. $$

05

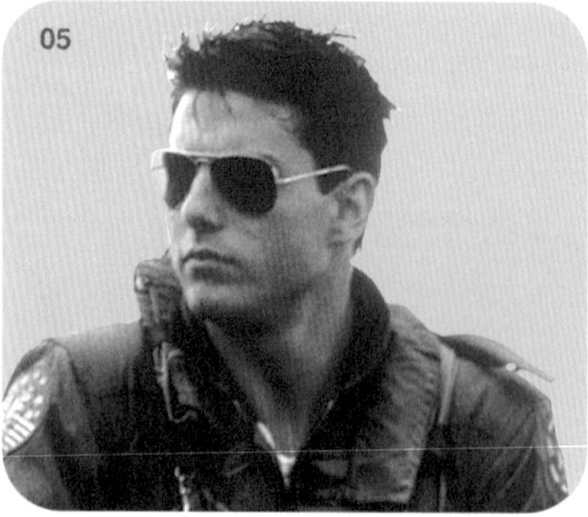

06

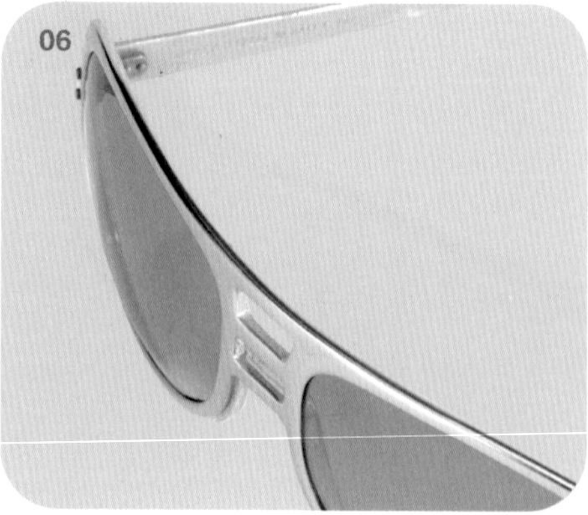

TIES

The 1940s are normally associated with wartime austerity, yet men's clothing of the period reminds us that – in America at least – things couldn't have been more different. In 1943, a group of Los Angeles teenagers called the zoot suits (for their billowing jackets and baggy narrow-bottomed trousers) clashed with local GIs over their fancy dress sense. Although neither the ensuing zoot suit riots nor subculture lasted long, the style quickly crept over to the American mainstream. In the immediate post-war period coats got longer, trousers fuller, and the neck tie simply went to another planet.

Size was the main difference; a narrow neck knot billowed down to five-inch wide silk and rayon canvases. Popular motifs of the time included Art Deco skyscrapers and Polynesian-style sunsets, while saucy pin-ups

01 Satin tie. Late 1940s.
Ⓢ Ⓢ Jane Mansfield
"peek-a-boo" rayon tie.
Late 1950s/early 1960s.
Ⓢ Ⓢ

02 Hand-painted palm
tree rayon tie. Late
1950s/early 1960s. Ⓢ
Hand-painted abstract
rayon tie. Late 1940s/
early 1950s. Ⓢ

✪ Salvador Dalí
"Blossoming Baroque"
satin tie. Late 1940s.
Ⓢ Ⓢ

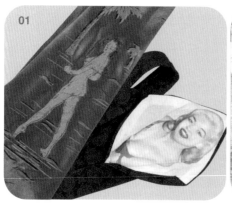

01

02

✪ **coolest** buy...

("peek-a-boos") were concealed on the reverse side. The gaudiest designs were known as "ham and eggs" because they camouflaged spilt breakfasts.

The pattern, often hand-painted, is the main selling point, but labels worth looking out for are Towncraft, Countess Mara, and Wembley. Van Heusen produced ties in three sizes, "Small, Medium, and Wow!"

✪ **coolest buy** Dalí ties

Salvador Dalí was an artist who had few hang-ups about selling out, and during his lifetime designed film sets for Hollywood and even licensed his own perfume. Signed rayon tie designs such as Flame of Time and Blossoming Baroque lend a touch of genius to the vintage 1940s tie.

JEWELLERY

With formal dress making a long-awaited comeback, the time for discovering vintage jewellery has never been better.

Cufflinks were originally worn after shirts with buttons came in, the cuff being the last part of the shirt that the wearer could adorn personally. Naturally they appealed to 19th-century English dandies such as Beau Brummel and Lord Byron. At formal occasions Brummel made sure that his cuffs – usually gold and mounted with gemstones – matched his tie pin.

The 1940s and 1950s were an equally extravagant time for men's fashion accessories. The main cufflink styles to look out for are enamel Art Deco, showy gold or silver with fake gems and visible outer cuff band, or exotic motifs such as Tiki and Aztec gods.

01 Bowling pin tie clip. Late 1950s. $$ Comedy/tragedy cufflinks and tie bar set. Early 1950s. $$

02 Enamel Deco cufflinks.1920s/1930s. $$ Mother of pearl Tiki cufflinks. 1950s. $

✪ Lenticular Man from U.N.C.L.E./ Apollo 12 cufflinks. 1960s images set in 1960s cufflinks; manufactured late 1980s. $

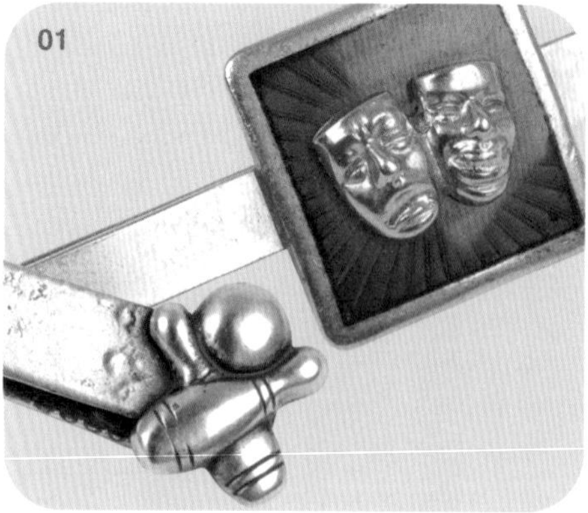

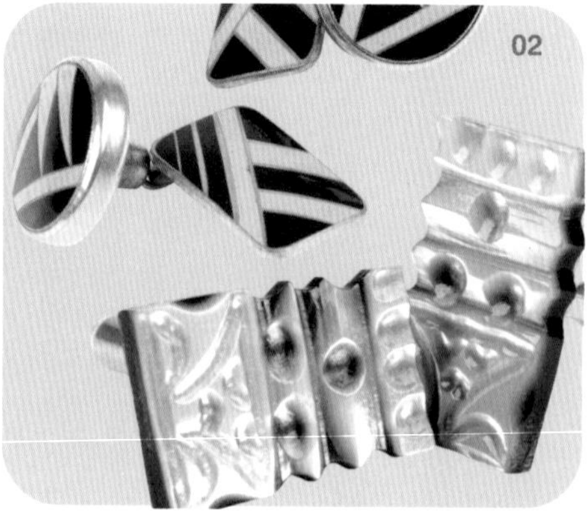

✪ coolest buy...

Tie bars and pins are also good buys and often come as part of a set alongside cufflinks. These should be boxed and in perfect condition.

✪ **coolest buy** Lenticular cufflinks

Believe it or not, lenticular 3-D images were highly impressive back in the 1950s and 1960s, appearing on anything from cereal boxes to political campaign stickers. The process was pioneered by American company VariVue in the 1940s, who later licensed their product worldwide.

The cufflinks above date from the late 1960s and the images are taken from comics depicting NASA space missions. Below are cuffinks based on *The Man From U.N.C.L.E.* James Bond has also starred on lenticular cufflinks.

MILITARIA

As previewed in the world's war zones, but also on fashion catwalks, military clothing is back with a bang. Military collectors are scouring boot sales and surplus shops for relics from two World Wars, Korea, Vietnam, and beyond.

Memorabilia from the German Third Reich and World War Two British commando divisions attract most attention and often the highest prices. Stylish as it may look, however, a 1930s Nazi officer's tunic is hardly the sort of thing that can be worn with pride.

Perhaps the most enduring and wearable military wear is that of the American GIs from World War Two onwards. Flying jackets like the brown horsehide A-2 bomber and its nylon replacement the MA-1 are timeless pieces that have been constantly rediscovered by fashion designers.

The A-2 first saw action in 1931 and was a US pilot's staple until 1942. The jacket has appeared in a number of guises and was even reintroduced to military service in the late 1980s. The ones to watch out for are made in the USA by Aero, Bronco, and Spiewak. Vintage A-2s in tip-top condition go for as much as £3,000 ($4,800).

MA-1s came into use during the 1950s. By then the jet age had arrived and pilots needed a more malleable, lightweight garment that also kept out freezing high-altitude temperatures. Alpha Industries supplied the USAF's original order, which came in sage green and midnight blue.

US Vietnam and Korean War memorabilia are gaining popularity with military collectors everywhere. Think *MASH* or *Apocalypse Now*.

01 M1 helmet with Mitchell pattern reversible cover and helmet band. Late 1960s. [$]

02 M1 helmet. Late 1960s. [$]

03 M1 helmet with woodland pattern cover and helmet band. Early 1970s. [$]

04 M1 helmet with Mitchell pattern reversible cover and helmet band. Late 1960s. [$]

124-125

Embroidered camouflaged shirts, authentic wide-brimmed "boonie" hats, and M1 helmets are in good supply. Another growing area of US forces memorabilia is sew-on patches, the best ones originating from airborne divisions or Special Forces units, some featuring snakes, skulls, and tigers.

When buying vintage military, be on your guard for reproductions and fakes. Make sure your dealer is reputable and ask for documents or letters of provenance if buying medals or other rare items.

✪ **coolest buy** Sukajan

After World War Two ended, American GIs still based in Japan would have souvenir jackets (*sukajan*) made up for them by local tailors. These satin bomber jackets were often reversible and hand painted and depicted local maps and USAF aircraft as well as traditional Japanese motifs such as dragons and tigers. Custom-made *sukajan* were also made for US military personnel in Korea, China, and Vietnam.

05 US military jacket. 1970s. $

06 Vietnam Special Forces pocket patch. Late 1960s. $$

✪ **Silk tour jacket from Japan. 1940s.** $$ **Nylon tour jacket from Vietnam. 1971.** $

05

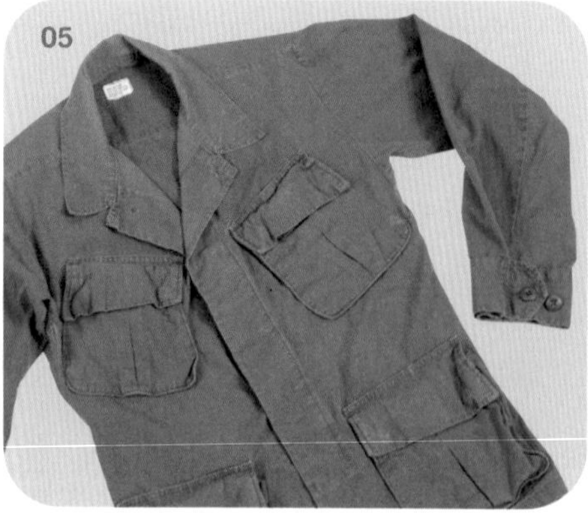

06

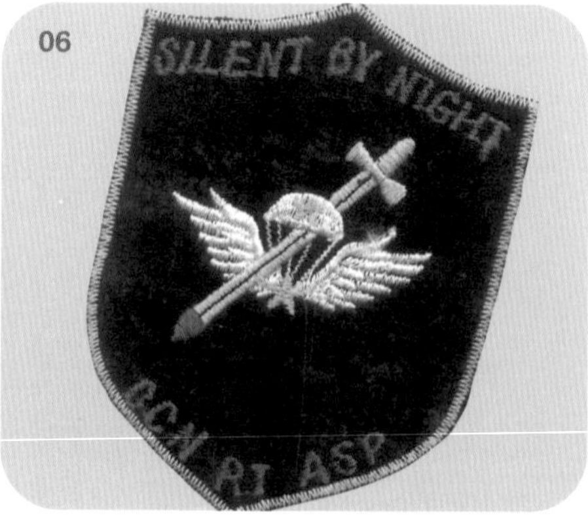

GO GO GO GO
GO GO GO GO
GO GO GO GO
GO GO GO GO

GO GO GO GO GO
GO GO GO GO
GO GO GO GO
GO GO GO GO

INTRODUCTION

When it comes to getting around, vehicles of the past can have modern variants lagging way behind. For pure adrenaline and black leather devil-may-care cool, no contemporary motorbike can match the apocalyptic shudder of an oily Norton or a chrome-covered Harley.

Although lacking the same raw power and head-turning capacity, classic Italian scooters and Japanese monkey bikes cannot be faulted on either economy or style.

Yesterday's bicycles are also worth long-overdue reappraisal. "Sit-up-and-beg" town bikes offer a graceful solution to urban congestion, while vintage Schwinn "muscle" bicycles vie for kerbside attention with Choppers and "old skool" BMXs.

For those who prefer to stay put, there are endless automotive trophies available, including old Jaguar club badges and Formula One race suits and helmets.

Small fortunes are also going up in the air with buyers lining up for relics attached to both moustachioed early aviators and jet age passenger flight, of which the much-missed Concorde currently commands most loyalty.

BIKES AND SCOOTERS

Motorcycles were developed towards the end of 19th century after a single combustion engine was applied to an ordinary bicycle. By the early 1900s the motorbike had achieved notoriety on the racing circuit and hundreds of small manufacturers, including Douglas, Indian, and Royal Enfield, joined this thriving industry.

Today the stage is dominated largely by the Japanese, but for a while the best road bikes in the world were made in Britain. Triumph's Bonneville, named after the Utah salt flats where Johnny Allen broke the world speed record in 1955, was produced in various forms from 1959 to 1989, and was the transport of choice for leather-clad "Ton-up boys" in the early 1960s.

BSA (Birmingham Small Arms Manufacturing) was the world's largest manufacturer of bikes after World War Two. BSA's Lightning and Spitfire, along with the 1952 Vincent Black Shadow, typify the classic Brit bike, while the BSA Gold Star was popular with race riders in the 1950s.

Norton also cleaned up on the racing circuit; their bikes won the Isle of Man TT repeatedly during the 1930s and 1940s. The Commando was the speed merchant's favourite between the late 1960s and the mid 1970s, and was voted "Machine of the Year" five times in succession.

Japan burst onto the scene in the 1970s, and bikes such as Kawasaki's Triple and the 1980 Suzuki Katana turned more than a few heads in their day. Japanese bikes were initially derided by purists, but owner clubs for 1980s Honda, Yamaha, and Suzuki are well-subscribed nowadays.

01 Triumph Bonneville. 649cc. 1970. $ $ $ $

02 BSA DB34 Gold Star. 499cc. 1956. $ $ $ $ $

03 Norton Commando, racing model. 745cc. 1971–4. $ $ $ $

04 Honda CB750 Four. 736cc. 1969. $ $ $ $

01

02

03

04

The scooter was an Italian phenomenon which surfaced shortly after World War Two. With old production lines ravaged, the Piaggio company came up with an economic two-wheeled vehicle aimed at both men and women that became known as the Vespa (Italian for wasp).

The Vespa GS 150 VS5 is one of the most sought-after models today. Built in the late 1950s, it features elegant styling with sporty 150cc engine. Innocenti's Lambretta was soon to join Piaggio in a post-war light motorcycle boom. Early models were crude and workmanlike, but the 1962 Lambretta Li series III marked an important shift towards scooter design. These sold in large numbers and were a huge commercial success for the company.

Harder to find in top condition are the Lambretta TV and SX series. These are the first production bikes to be fitted with front disc brakes. The later SX model (1966–9) had improved styling with a speedo dial that went up to 90mph. Scooter fans collect practically anything to do with the Vespa

05 Suzuki Katana.
1000cc. 1983. $$$$$$$$

06 Ducati 900SS.
864cc. 1979. $$$$$$$$

134-135 BIKES AND SCOOTERS

or Lambretta name, including old advertising, owner manuals, club memo-rabilia, and pennants.

Despite obvious limitations on the road, miniature bikes such as the Honda Monkey and its successor the Dax attract growing interest from collectors. There is even a custom mini bike scene, especially in Japan.

Known as the Monkey for making riders appear simian, the Honda CZ100 was the first Japanese mini bike to be exported in the early 1960s. With tiny 50cc engine and 5-inch tyres, it was meant as a fun beginner's bike that could be stored in car, truck, or mobile home.

The Dax, which didn't reach Europe until 1970, came with a bigger 70cc engine and had a seat designed for two. Many colour and design varia-tions appeared before Honda stopped production in the late 1990s.

Buying a classic bike or scooter requires similar principles to classic car buying, so subscribe to specialist magazines, improve your knowledge, and, if necessary, join a member's club. Before paying out check all the

Ducati – Italian for super bike

With their unrivalled European sports pedigree and talented in-house designer Fabio Taglioni, Ducati introduced the world to Italian super bikes.

The four-stroke 750SS had trademark twin single engines and rocketed to 120mph, while the 900SS, launched in 1976, competed with the best of the new Japanese super bikes and could notch 140mph.

This stunning bike's racing credentials were further enhanced when Mike Hailwood came out of retirement to win the Isle of Man TT on a tuned version.

relevant paperwork. Fakes and reproductions (especially with old BSAs) are common. Be particularly suspicious if the engine and frame serial numbers don't match.

✪ **coolest buy** Harley-Davidson

Of the classic American machines, Harley-Davidson (and to a lesser extent Indian) are the only names that really interest the collector. Harleys were ridden long and hard by the original Hell's Angels in the 1940s and 1950s and starred in the 1969 film *Easy Rider*. Today, "the hog" epitomizes a somewhat safer rock 'n' roll rebellion.

Rare examples can fetch as much as £100,000 ($160,000), and unlike some makes they hold their value extremely well. The Electra Glide captures the best of the classic post-war Harleys; trademark V-twin engine, white-walled tyres, cushioned long-haul saddle, and enough chrome to dazzle a Ray-Ban wearing traffic cop.

07 Vespa GS 150 VS1. 148cc. 1955. $$$$

08 Honda CZ100. 49cc. 1963–70. $$$$

✪ Harley-Davidson Electra Glide. 1200cc. 1965. $$$$$

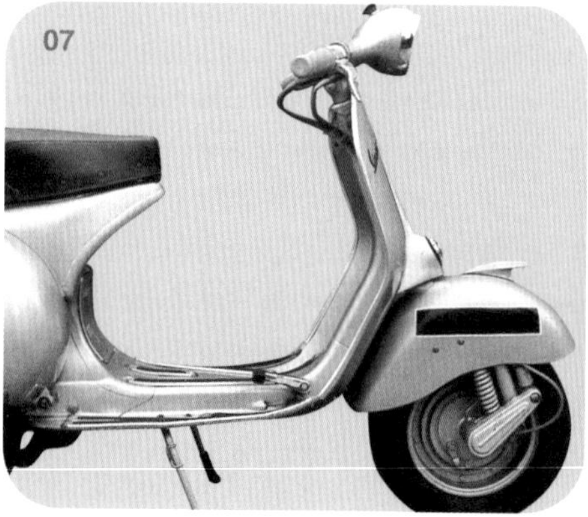

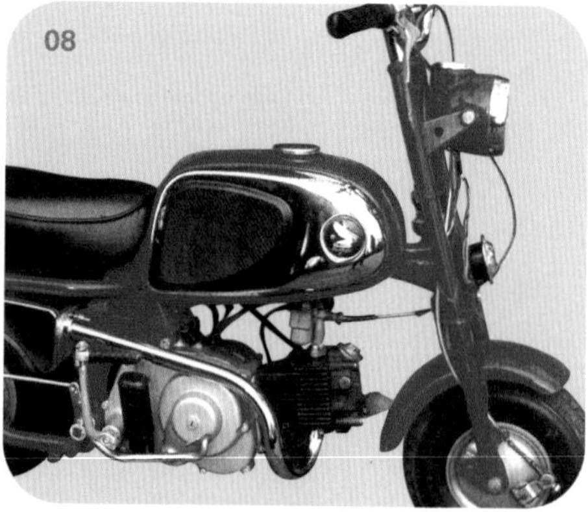

✪ **coolest** buy...

BICYCLES

--➤

At the end of the 19th century, bicycle riding was a booming leisure activity backed by a substantial manufacturing base. The arrival of the car made it a more specialist form of transport, however, be it in the Tour de France or on a cobbled Cambridge quad.

Stylish "old black bicycles" made by Hercules, Rudge, or Raleigh can be picked up for less than £100, although a 1930s Lea Francis gentlemen's bicycle recently fetched over £1,000 ($1,600) at auction.

Chicago-based Schwinn began making bicycles in 1895 and pioneered the streamlined style normally associated with classic American cars and motorcycles. The Black Phantom came out in 1949 and became one of the best-selling bicycles in America. Riders could be excused for thinking that it was a motorcycle; it had white-walled balloon tyres, mock oil tank with solid-looking chrome fenders, and weighed a ton by today's standards.

The 1960s saw the arrival of the "muscle bike", and Schwinn led the way with the 1963 Sting-Ray and the 1968 Krates. Sporting ape-hanger bars and long banana seats, these lent themselves readily to customising. Schwinn also sold chrome horns, speedos, and mirrors to help riders on their way.

Children brought up in Britain during the 1970s and 1980s will have memories of another mean-looking two-wheeler, the Raleigh Chopper. Highly influenced by the *Easy Rider* motorcycle fad, this Nottingham-made cult classic sold well on both sides of the pond.

Both mark one and the superior mark two versions are collector's items, the most prized being the special edition 1977 Silver Jubilee with silver

Raleigh Chopper II.
1972. $$$

BRITISH
originality

Once there were ships. Then there were aircraft. Now there is Hovercraft, a whole new way of zipping across the sea – at high speed. It's this sort of original thinking that puts Raleigh out in front too, with innovations that really take off.

metallic finish. Others to watch out for are the Sprint, which came with curled race-style bars, and a five-speed version available in bright pink.

The rise of BMX sports bikes eventually saw off the Chopper. Hutch Trickstars and Torker Cruisers ruled the BMX scene of the 1980s, and unlikely as it may sound, "old skool" BMXs are becoming highly sought after today.

✪ **coolest buy** The Bowden Spacelander

Automotive designer Benjamin Bowden's Spacelander fibreglass bicycle was born out of the 1946 Britain Can Make It exhibition and featured chainless shaft-driven ride mechanism and energy-storing hub dynamo.

Widely considered too costly to mass produce, it was eventually put into production by Bombard Industries Inc. in Michigan, USA, although only 500 or so were made before a law suit forced the company into liquidation.

The Spacelander became a collector's item in the 1980s. Since then prices for this space age rarity have rocketed up to £15,000 ($24,000).

02 Schwinn Apple Krate. New old stock accessories. 1969.
$ $ $ $

03 Schwinn Ramshorn Fastback. 1967.
$ $ $

✪ Bowden Spacelander. 1959.
$ $ $ $ $

140-141 BICYCLES

AUTOMOBILIA

Whether the allegiance is to Mini or Maserati, motoring enthusiasts can express their passion for their car's heritage in a number of ways.

One of the most evocative reminders of past motoring glories is the club badge, once proudly bolted onto almost every vehicle's front grille. Today most badge collectors stick to car model or preferred motoring organization. The AA, for example, have been around since 1905 and have therefore produced a wide and interesting selection of badge designs over the years.

Original motor manuals and sales brochures – especially for high-performance cars – make a good start to any automobilia collection. You can also find mint oil and spark plug stickers, showroom display cards, and adverts from back issues of magazines such as *Autocar* and *Motor*.

The world of motor racing is one of the most exciting arenas for automobilia hunters; the most sought-after items include driver helmets and race suits. Signed items worn by legendary names such as Ayrton Senna and James Hunt fetch the highest prices, although items worn by current F1 drivers also make good investments.

Motor racing has hardly gone unnoticed by Hollywood and original promotional posters from auto-centric movies like Steve McQueen's *Le Mans* and *Bullitt* are snapped up quicker today than a Ford Mustang speeding through a San Francisco junction. Other movie posters starring iconic cars are Paul Newman's *Winning* and *Vanishing Point*.

Although cars didn't feature highly in them, Shell travel posters from the 1930s have become highly valuable of late for their idealized

01 Esso "I've got a tiger in my tank" promotional material. 1960s. $

02 Ford Mustang brochure. 1967. $

03 Paul Nash poster for Shell. 1936. $$$

04 Japanese *Le Mans* film poster. 1971. $$

01

I'VE GOT A 🐯 IN MY TANK

PLAY SAFE—PLAY IN YOUR GARDEN OR PARK

PUT A TIGER IN YOUR TANK

JIG-SAW

A S.A.V.E. THE TIGER

02

Three new ways to answer the call of the Mustang...

Mustang '67

03

TO VISIT BRITAIN'S LANDMARKS

KIMMERIDGE FOLLY, DORSET   PAUL NASH

YOU CAN BE SURE OF SHELL

04

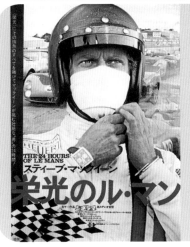

THE 24 HOURS OF LE MANS

スティーブ・マックイーン

栄光のル・マン

representations of the English countryside painted by artists such as Graham Sutherland and Paul Nash.

Shell and their competitors Esso were involved in some memorable promotional duels in the 1960s and 1970s. Esso's "Put a tiger in your tank" campaign came with an array of now highly collectible merchandising including tiger key fobs, bumper stickers, and a novelty tiger tail that you attached to your petrol tank.

✪ **coolest buy** Petrol pump globes

For anyone nostalgic for the smell of old petrol station forecourts and the sight of flat-capped pump attendants, how about branded plastic or glass globes from pumps that have long been consigned to the recycling plant?

These come in a variety of shapes and sizes and sport names that may mean little to the modern motorist. Bulb-lit petrol globes (original, not one of the many American-style reproductions) look great practically anywhere.

05 Gerhard Berger race helmet, signed. 1997. $$$$

06 Emerson Fittipaldi postcard, signed. 1978. $

✪ **Assorted US petrol globes. 1950s–60s.** $$–$$$

05

06

✪ **coolest** buy...

AERONAUTICA

Man first mastered powered, sustained, and controlled flight about 100 years ago, yet experiments in flying began hundreds of years earlier, giving the aeronautica enthusiast early ballooning, gliders, or perhaps even the Wright Brothers as possible focuses for their collection.

The early 20th century sparked some significant developments in aviation, notably Louis Bleriot's first flight across the Channel and the early fighter plane, which first saw action high over World War One trenches.

Wartime has proved to be a rich seam for aviation memorabilia, with particular attention paid to anything linked to World War One aces such as the Red Baron or famous airborne offensives like the 1943 Dambusters Raid. Leather flying helmets, logbooks, wooden propeller blades, and commemorative cigarette cases all fetch top prices at auction.

With so many to choose from, "firsts" also are a favourite subject; such memorabilia might include letters written by Bleriot or signed Chuck Yeager photographs commemorating his 1947 breaking of the "sound barrier".

Famous long-distance flyers and pre-war celebrities such as Amy Johnson and Charles Lindberg still have a big following and items relating to their greatest achievements go for thousands today. Recently, however, it is the golden age of passenger flight that has caught the imagination. Up until the 1960s, flying was the expensive preserve of the so-called "jet set". In-flight ephemera such as flight bags, luggage labels, menus, cutlery, ashtrays, playing cards, and sick bags are popular, as are company desk models of Boeing 707 and 747s.

01 Amy Johnson commemorative booklet. 1930s. [$]

02 World War II squadron leader's hat. 1939–45. [$]

03 World War II RAF Mark VIII goggles. 1939–45. [$]

04 Card signed by Charles Lindbergh. 1930–50. [$][$]

146-147

Swissair, BOAC, and TWA are among the most collectible airlines, but items bearing the logo of exotic or long-defunct airlines such as Imperial Airways (who ran a luxury flying boat service) are also sought after. Tickets or timetables from the trans-continental classic routes remain a wise buy. Airline posters have taken off over the last few years too; choose from colonial sea planes and palm trees to the 1960s abstract approach of BOAC or Pan Am.

✪ **coolest buy** Concorde memorabilia

Between 1969 and 2003, this iconic supersonic passenger jet wowed earthly onlookers on both sides of the Atlantic. Pieces that have come up for auction include cockpit instruments such as the Mach visual display unit, which helped record speeds of 1,350mph (twice the speed of sound). Concorde cabin seats, ashtrays, and stationery – especially from the later Terence Conran refit – have changed hands for significant sums, while the more technically inclined bid for prototype sketches and scale models.

05 Pan American Airways luggage label. 1930s. $

06 British European Airways bag. 1960s. $

✪ Concorde memorabilia. Jigsaw, model, brochure and in-flight safety card. All early 1970s. $

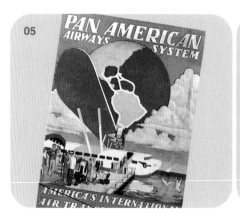

☆ **coolest** buy...

UNDS SOUND
S SOUNDS SO
UNDS SOUND:
S SOUNDS SO

SOUNDS SOUNDS SOU
UNDS SOUNDS
SOUNDS SOU
UNDS SOUNDS

INTRODUCTION

From jazz to rock 'n' roll, hip-hop, and beyond, music plays a dominant role in our cultural lives. Musically minded collectors might wish to survey the gleaming hardware on offer in our idealized vintage music store. There are beautiful solid-bodied and semi-acoustic American guitars mythologized by old blues men and rock revivalists alike, as well as pioneering Moog and Prophet synthesizers which helped give rock a new dimension in the 1970s and 1980s.

For those who prefer just listening, try dropping a dime or two into the classic American jukebox, an invention that started in the humble "juke joint" and ended up a major moneyspinner in the youth-orientated 1950s. With sales of vinyl on the rise again, the jukebox is very much back in demand; this time as a cool retro household object that you can actually use.

Pop fans don't go empty-handed either. Billboard posters, stage wear, fanzines, badges, and rare picture disks are just some of the attractions of the memorabilia circuit. For those prepared to pay, that rare collarless Beatle jacket or Eminem baseball cap is yours.

GUITARS

The electric guitar has been around since 1930s jazz guitarists tried amplifying their hollow-bodied instruments to keep up with the volume levels of fellow band members.

Gibson manufactured the "electric Spanish" ES-150 model in 1936, but the solid-bodied electric guitar with bolt-on neck and electric pick-ups didn't appear until the 1950s. Fender, founded by Leo Fender in the 1940s, claimed this milestone with the 1951 Telecaster. Still in production today, and played by the likes of Keith Richards and Joe Strummer, the earliest prototype versions were called the Broadcaster. These are extremely rare today and fetch peak prices whenever they come up for auction.

Fender followed the Telecaster with the fretted Precision bass guitar, an instrument that almost overnight replaced wieldy double-basses in American rhythm and blues bands. Look for models made in the late 1950s with split-coil pick-ups and maple necks.

Not to be outdone by Fender's solid-bodied successes, Gibson responded with Les Paul in 1952. This ever-popular guitar came in four models: Junior, Special, Standard, and Custom. The Custom version of 1954 is known as the "black beauty" and came with gold-plated fittings and "Tune-o-matic" bridge. The "LP" went on to define the sound of glam, country rock, and heavy metal in the 1970s.

Other Gibsons worth getting your fingers on are late 1950s thinlines, especially the ES-335, a semi-hollow electric associated with Chuck Berry and BB King. Models made around 1959 with dot necks are the most collectible.

01 Gibson Les Paul Standard. 1968. $$$$

02 Fender Esquire. 1955. $$$$$

03 Gibson ES-335 TD. 1959. $$$$$

04 Gretsch White Falcon. 1967. $$$$

154-155

01

02

03

04

Incredibly, the Gibson Flying V goes back to the same age, but aroused little interest until prog rockers saw its potential in the 1970s. This monster axe was produced in limited numbers with a Korina wood body until 1963. A mahogany version, which Jimi Hendrix performed with, came out in the late 1960s, while in the early 1980s the Flying V returned as a heritage line.

The 1950s electric guitar boom coincided nicely with the dawn of rock 'n' roll, and soon other manufacturers were jumping onto the bandwagon. Gretsch, a family-run firm which had been making guitars and drums since the beginning of the century, were the first to bring in custom colour finishes. Gretsch guitars in pearl white or Cadillac green echoed the gleaming fin-tailed cars in car showrooms, and were quickly adopted by stars such as Eddie Cochran and Duane Eddy.

The 1955 White Falcon (model 6136), featuring single cutaway body with gold finish and pearl fingerboard inlays, was by far the most dazzling piece in the music shop window. Retailing at $600, it was strictly for rockers who

05 Gibson Flying V. 1958. $$$$$

06 Hofner 500/1 "Violin" Bass. 1963. $$$$

had hits in the charts or a Caddy in the garage. A mint condition vintage Gretsch costs considerably more today.

Although responsible for some of the finest valve-driven amplifiers, British guitar manufacturers have been few and far between. One, Burns of London, defies this preconception.

The driving force of the late Jim Burns, Burns became known for their space age-style models in the early 1960s. In their heyday (1960–65), Burns's homespun company was making roughly 150 guitars a week, some ending up in the hands of beat bands like The Searchers and The Tornados. Today the Burns name lives on with reissues inscribed with the legendary "Burns of London". Among the most wanted original models are the Double Six and the Black Bison, a stunning piece in any age, and of which only 49 were made.

Serious collectors of vintage electric guitars always go for the cleanest, most original examples in their factory cases. Stickers, spray paint, and

The Beatle bass

German violin and guitar makers Hofner might have played little part in rock 'n' roll history were it not for a young Paul McCartney going into a Hamburg guitar shop and parting his hard-earned cash for a Hofner 500/1 hollow-bodied "violin" bass.

As a left-handed player he chose the instrument primarily because its symmetrical shape didn't present a problem when turning it round the other way. With Paul's patronage and the later success of the Fab Four, the guitar soon became known as the "Beatle bass".

chips in the bodywork seriously reduce their value. Vintage American-made guitars are generally hard to replicate, although there have been cases of newish Fender necks being bolted onto vintage bodies. Never buy a guitar unless you've sat down with it and heard it sing.

✪ **coolest buy** Fender Stratocaster

When this guitar came out in 1954, it put all other models in the shade. The comfortable sculpted body, three pick-ups, recessed jack socket, and handy vibrato arm made it an instant hit with players. Legends who have dallied with this axe include Buddy Holly, Eric Clapton, and Jimi Hendrix, who strung his right-handed Strat for a left-hander, even setting fire to one at the 1967 Montery Pop Festival.

Buyers should look for pre-1966 models, made before CBS bought the company and mass produced them with disappointing results. Find one with original tweed flight case and play through an old Fender valve amp.

07 Fender Precision Bass. 1962. $$$$

08 Burns Bison Bass. Mid 1960s. $$$$

✪ **Fender Stratocasters. Red Eric Clapton signature model. 1987.** $$$$ **White finish. 1965.** $$$$$ **Blue sparkle finish. 1964.** $$$$$

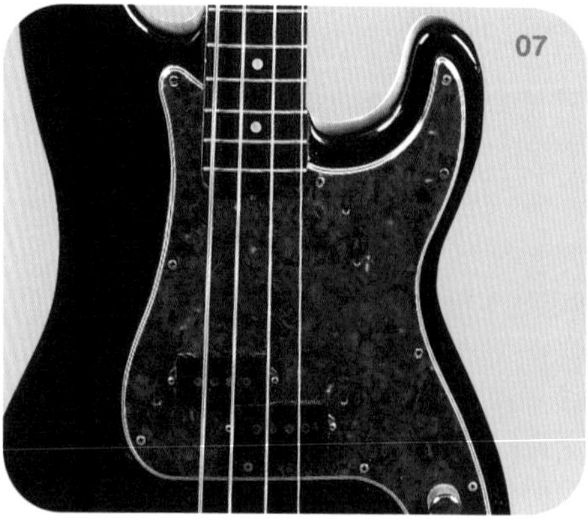
07

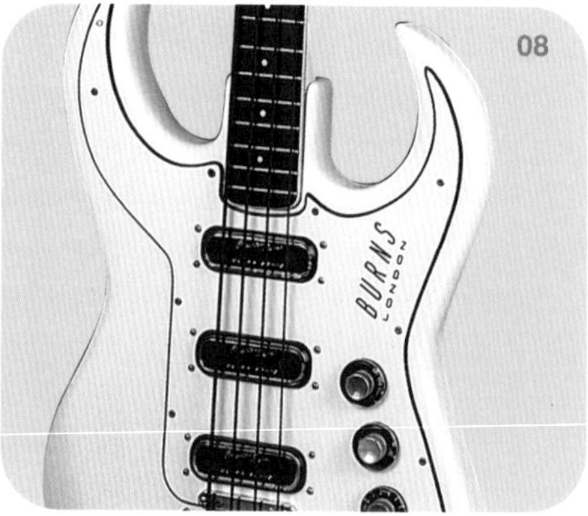

08

✪ **coolest** buy...

SYNTHS

--→

Before digital technology revolutionized music making in the mid 1980s, the analogue synthesizer was the sound of rock's avant garde. Brian Eno, Kraftwerk, and other clever types played them, but to the average punter they may well have come from a NASA control centre. Now a new generation of musicians are rediscovering them, putting an ever-increasing price tag on the synth's more seminal moments.

One of the earliest and most collectible is the British-made Mellotron Model 300. Years before sampling had been invented, the Mellotron's keyboard could play taped analogue recordings of acoustic instruments such as flutes, strings, or a boys' choir. This 1960s synth can be heard on The Beatles "Strawberry Fields Forever" and Led Zeppelin's "The Rain Song". Mark II versions (the 400) were purchased by the BBC for *Dr Who*'s famous sound effects department.

An American, Bob Moog (that's Moog as in vogue), was the first person to manufacture analogue synths for the mass market. Former physics student Moog first cut his teeth in electronic engineering by making transistorized theremins, the hand-operated device invented by Dr Leon Theremin in the 1920s and used most notably in horror film soundtracks.

Surprisingly compact and affordable, his Minimoog (see Coolest Buy) has a distinctive fat, warm sound that over the years has appealed to musicians as diverse as Herbie Hancock, Air, and The Chemical Brothers.

Moog produced a number of other groundbreaking synths in the 1970s, including the portable Moog Sonic Six and the polyphonic Polymoog (it

Mellotron Model 400.
Rare clear acrylic
version. 1971.
$$$$$

could play more than one note at a time). ELP's Keith Emerson boasted the biggest modular stage set-up of all; his custom Moog stood 4ft 6in high and weighed 550lb – every roadie's nightmare!

Weighing in at a hefty 220lb, the Yamaha CS-80 is one of the rarest synths around. Armed with 22 preset sounds, it was polyphonic and had a pitch bend ribbon controller. The CS-80 was played by Stevie Wonder in the 1970s. Only 2,000 examples were made before production stopped in 1979.

Sequential's Prophet 5 (made between 1978 and 1984) once had the punchiest bass notes and the silkiest string sections; it was also the first polyphonic synth to be equipped with a memory. Prophet 5s and 10s helped shape the sound of Talking Heads and New Order, and with the renewed influence of 1980s music, these look like a good bet again.

The early 1980s were an exciting time for the synthesizer, with many new manufacturers joining this booming industry. Roland, who are a Japanese firm despite the name, were responsible for the first Japanese-

02 Moog Polymoog.
1976. $\circledS\circledS\circledS$

03 Yamaha CS-80.
1978. $\circledS\circledS\circledS\circledS$

made keyboard synth, the SH-1000. Roland launched the eight-voice polyphonic Jupiter 8 in 1980, and it soon became a staple for 1980s synth merchants such as The Human League and Giorgio Moroder. Beating its competitors hands down, the Jupiter 8 also boasted a 61-note keyboard and 64-patch memory.

Around the same time Roland introduced the TB-303 combined sequencer and bass machine. Not only consigning legions of drummers and bass players to the pop wilderness, this once-cheap gadget helped launch the "acid house" movement at the end of the decade.

Old analogue synths made by an engineer on a workbench have far more personality than their digital counterparts. Some of the earliest synths are beautifully finished in wood and have colour-coded dial displays, sometimes even screens, that can keep owners up for hours.

No two identical models ever sound the same, and they will often require a warm-up before playing. Before buying a vintage synthesizer, make sure it

Bark to the future

Fairlight's CMI (Computer Musical Instrument) arrived in 1980 and had a price tag of up to $25,000 ($40,000). Despite orders from Peter Gabriel and Stevie Wonder, few musicians knew what this multi-pieced monster was, let alone how to play it.

Perhaps the Fairlight's main contribution to synthesizer history is that it could store 1Mb of recorded data on an eight-inch floppy disk, making it the first mass-marketed digital sampler. Included among the CMI's sampled sounds was a barking dog which belonged to one of Fairlight's programmers.

has had a thorough service. This can cost up to £300 ($480) but it's well worth it; years of inactivity can make an old synth go completely out of tune.

✪ **coolest buy** The Minimoog

Having equipped Brian Eno and Keith Emerson with custom synths, Bob Moog and his team decided to develop a compact performance synthesizer that could be programmed without mind-boggling patch cords.

The Minimoog first appeared in 1972 and must have baffled keyboard players with its mini banks of oscillators and modifiers. Moog designed his baby for use in the recording studio or at gigs. Special features include a fold-up control panel and wheel-controlled pitch and modulation.

As with many products that are ahead of their time, sales were initially slow. That was until *Miami Vice* composer Jan Hammer came along and developed his distinctive guitar sound on it. It also plays mean bass lines and remains a studio and performance favourite to this day.

04 Roland Jupiter 8. 1982. [$][$][$][$]

05 Roland TB-303. 1982. [$][$][$]

✪ Moog Minimoog. 1970. [$][$][$][$]

04

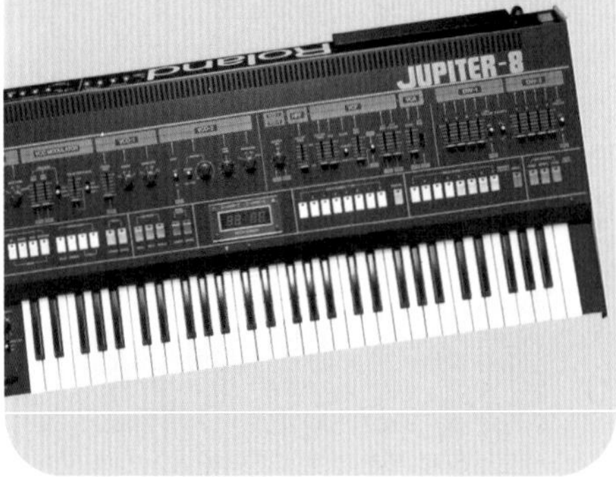

05

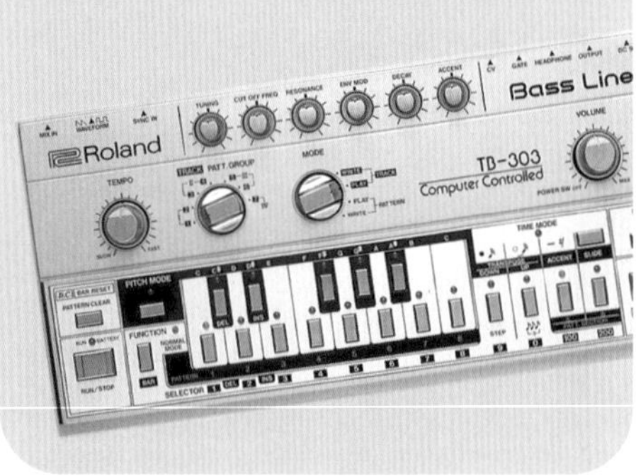

JUKEBOXES

-->

Although the jukebox is popularly associated with the crackling, slightly jumpy sound of Elvis and Gene Vincent records, the first coin-operated music machines were to be found decades earlier in American "juke joints". The word "juke" comes from African-American slang meaning evil; visitors to roadside juke joints obligingly dropped a dime or two into the jukebox to hear the latest blues recordings.

Early designs were based on the phonograph and were later influenced by the styling of the domestic radio. Compared to later jukeboxes, these were heavy and not especially decorative. After Prohibition ended, however, the jukebox became a big money-spinner with designers giving them illuminated fronts and dancing bubble features. Models like the 1941 Rock-Ola Spectravox were nothing less than musical Art Deco towers.

Legendary jukebox designer Paul Fuller worked for Wurlitzer, USA in the 1930s and 1940s, creating classic Wurlitzer models such as the 700 and the 1100. The 1015, released in 1946, was the most popular of its day and has been much copied since. With its maple veneer frame, coloured bubble tubes, and cast metal fittings, original versions are easy enough to identify.

Wurlitzer first made their name as makers of player pianos and theatre organs, but their jukeboxes are known for their distinctive carousel mechanisms, first showcased on the 1954 1700 model. This allowed the 45rpm discs to be clearly viewed as they played in a vertical position.

Wurlitzer's rivals Seeburg introduced Select-O-Matic on their machines in 1948, offering customers 100 selections (both sides of 50 selected

Wurlitzer 800. 24 selections. 1940.
Ⓢ Ⓢ Ⓢ Ⓢ

discs). They also produced the first jukebox to play 45rpm singles (the Seeburg M100B). Previously jukeboxes had been stacked with the larger 78s, but luckily for Seeburg, it was the single that emerged as the standard format for the new rock 'n' roll market.

By the 1950s, most jukeboxes were drawing their inspiration from automobile design or the era's obsession with space travel. AMi's L200 model, produced in 1958, beautifully mirrors the chrome front grille and bumper of a 1950s Dodge or Oldsmobile, while its curved glass upper body is practically a windscreen. Rock-Ola, the coin-op machine company started by one David C. Rockola in the 1920s, had the Rocket and the Fireball, while Chantal Ltd of Bristol produced a now very rare model called the Meteor.

The idiosyncratic Chantal jukebox was also made in Switzerland and France, although production was limited due to factory fires. Chantal juke-boxes are notoriously difficult to restore and maintain and are therefore better suited to the true enthusiast.

02 Wurlitzer 1700. 104 selections. 1954.
$$$$$

03 AMi L200. 200 selections. 1958.
$$$$$

Sadly, by the mid 1960s jukeboxes were on the way out. Stereo had arrived and a more affluent and independently minded young generation were listening to long-player albums in the comfort of their own home. Designs from the jukebox's declining years, such as the 1975 Rock-Ola 464, demonstrated a more minimalist approach with faux neon light panels harking back to the 1950s. Jukeboxes from the 1970s are generally cheaper to buy, yet have identical running costs to those from the golden age (late 1930s to early 1960s).

Another nostalgic and highly desirable jukebox, the Wurlitzer 1050 appears to be from the 1940s, although it was actually made in 1973. Wurlitzer made only 1,600 of these plastic-bodied machines before going out of business shortly afterwards.

Nostalgia remains the main reason why jukeboxes are still in demand today. A slightly scratched vinyl 45 played through an old jukebox valve amplifier is an experience that modern systems simply cannot replicate.

Jukeboxes on the screen

Since a brief appearance in *The Wild One*, the jukebox has often been wheeled onto film and television sets to evoke 1950s America. Popular 1970s TV series *Happy Days* used a Seeburg M100C in the title sequence, but in Arnold's café "the Fonz" was way too cool ever to put a dime in; he got his favourite selections played by pounding the jukebox with his fist. *Grease*, which starred John Travolta and Olivia Newton John, made good use of a 1973 Wurlitzer 1050, while in *Ghost*, a 1960s AMi Continental plays "Unchained Melody" during Demi Moore and Patrick Swayze's potter's wheel scene.

Before letting a jukebox into your home, make sure the vendor offers you a period of warranty. With old ones things will always go wrong, so be prepared for a few bills along the way. That said, in jukebox land one play costs just 10 cents, so be sure to have a pile of dimes ready and enjoy.

✪ coolest buy AMi Continental

Just before AMi (Automatic Musical Instrument Co) merged with vending giants Rowe International, they launched the now highly sought-after Continental. Designed by Jack R. Mell, it featured 100 selections under a glass bubble display and curved selection panel. "Truly the style of tomorrow, for more play today", boasted ads from the early 1960s.

The 1961 Continental is perhaps the ultimate space-age jukebox, and unsurprisingly became known in coffee bars as "the radar". Both mark 1 and 2 models fetch good prices, the later having the advantage of an improved trim and add-on stereo unit.

04 Rock Ola 1434 Super Rocket. 50 selections. 1951–2. $$$$$

05 Chantal Meteor (British example). 200 selections. 1959. $$$$$

✪ AMi Continental II. 200 selections. 1962. $$$$

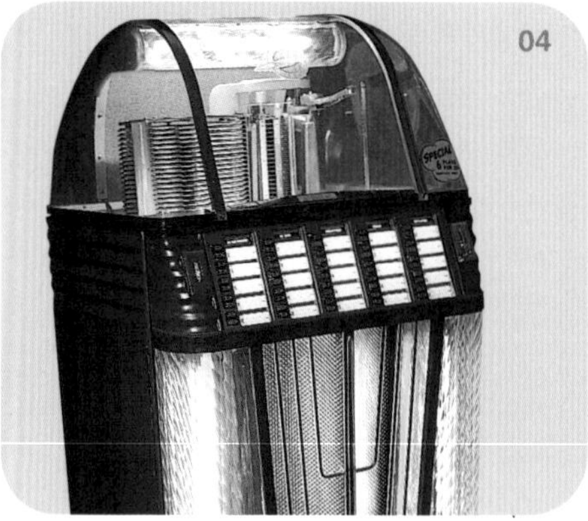

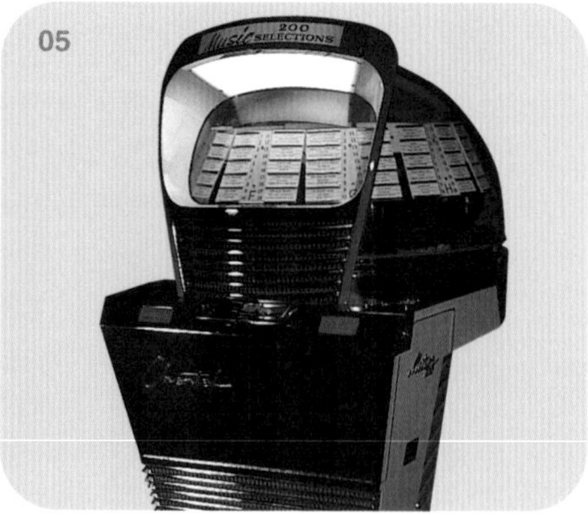

ROCK COLLECTIBLES

Rock and pop memorabilia is becoming an integral part of the collecting scene, with the first high-profile auctions going back to the 1980s. John Lennon's psychedelic Rolls Royce famously sold for \$2.3 million in 1985, although top prices have also been paid for a pair of drumsticks signed by Led Zeppelin's John Bonham and the custom bass guitar collection belonging to the late John Entwistle of The Who.

As worn by the stars themselves, stage clothes are amongst the most desirable pieces. Elvis Presley stage wear and accessories are especially prized in the US. Prices of his 1970s jump suits, belts, and medallions are sky high, but then again, there was only one King.

In the glam rock era, stars such as Brian Ferry and Roxy Music had their stage clothes made by Anthony Price and legendary London boutique Mr Freedom. 1970s Ferry trademark short zip-up jackets and GI shirts are bona fide glam rock classics, as are Elton John's custom platform shoes.

Original punk fashion also has a growing following, and items worn by its standard bearers Johnny Rotten and Joe Strummer have their price too. Rotten's mohair sweater and "Anarchy" shirt designed by Vivienne Westwood and Malcolm McLaren have traded hands for thousands.

Instruments played by famous dead musicians such as Jimi Hendrix and Kurt Cobain have a special attraction in the market. Hendrix was known for his explosive live performances, and even his battered Fender Stratocasters have value. Signed guitars from legends such as John Lee Hooker and

01 Angus Young of AC/DC's school boy stage outfit. 1980s. [\$][\$][\$][\$]

02 Dave Hill of Slade's boots. 1970s. [\$][\$]

03 John Lennon's Chelsea boots. 1960s. [\$][\$][\$][\$][\$]

04 Vivienne Westwood knitted mohair sweater worn by Johnny Rotten of the Sex Pistols. Late 1970s. [\$][\$][\$][\$]

172-173

Jimmy Page command similar levels of excitement, although buyers must be sure of authenticity.

The most collectible name of all, however, is The Beatles. Fans will shell out small fortunes for practically anything connected to the Fab Four, including rough set lists, lyrics, concert tickets, limited edition Apple merchandise, even a bath tub from John Lennon's Ascot home. On an average day, online trading sites will offer anything from rare Beatles promo discs to handwritten letters from Beatles manager Brian Epstein.

Original works by British pop artist Peter Blake for the seminal 1967 *Sergeant Pepper* album count as both pop memorabilia and fine art. Blake was commissioned to design the album's famous cover montage – for a one-off fee of £200 ($320) – and works that have come up for auction since include cut-out heads, life-sized blow-ups, and at least two versions of the *Sergeant Pepper* drum skin. Blake later designed album covers for Band Aid's "Do They Know It's Christmas?" and Paul Weller's *Stanley Road*.

05 Foil printed poster by Martin Sharp. 1967. $$

06 Poster for Jimi Hendrix at the Filmore and Winterland by Rick Griffin. 1968. $$$$

05

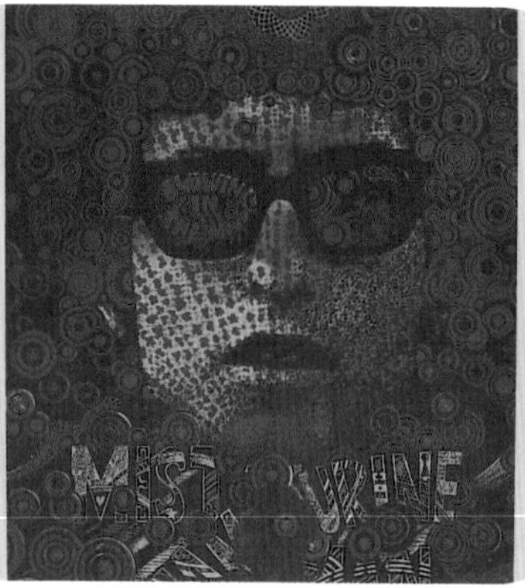

06

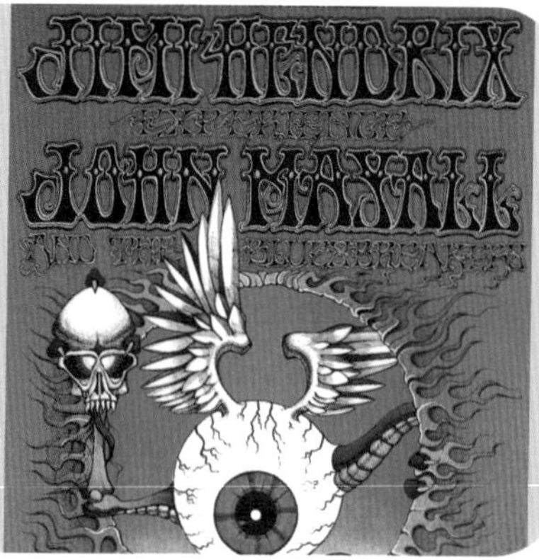

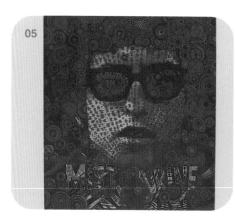

Graphic artist Jamie Reid's work with the Sex Pistols is no less significant a contribution to rock 'n' roll art, and prices for Reid's original posters, flyers, and other Sex Pistols artwork reflect this. Reid, a former art school pal of Malcolm McLaren, conjured up the band's cut-and-paste logo and the banned "God Save The Queen" single cover with the defaced image of Her Majesty.

Collectors of punk memorabilia might also consider items relating to other important bands of the era. Why not focus on The Buzzcocks, Wire, or The Ramones? In 1977 a British punk fanzine told readers "Here's a chord, here's another one... now form a band." Crude, photocopied productions like Mark Perry's *Sniffin' Glue* were distributed at legendary punk venues such as The Roxy and The Vortex, although their cover value is somewhat higher today. More affordable but no less evocative of the period are small pin badges of new wave and post-punk bands like The Specials or Joy Division.

The rock poster takes a trip

In the early days, rock 'n' roll concert posters would echo the variety show billboard. Emerging bands like the Rolling Stones or The Animals shared the bill with six or seven other acts, all represented in a straightforward graphic style. By the mid 1960s, however, the rock poster started to take its own direction, with young graphic artists such as Martin Sharp and Rick Griffin developing a style that was loosely described as "psychedelic art". Original silkscreen posters from the late 1960s/early 1970s era are highly collectible, especially those promoting legendary events such as Woodstock.

✪ **coolest buy** Vinyl

Vinyl is an infinitely deep mine for the pop memorabilia collector. Amongst the rarest, most collectible discs are A&M's limited edition pressing of "Anarchy in the UK" and EMI's in-house promo of "Bohemian Rhapsody". You don't have to fork out thousands to become a vinyl junkie, however, and a world of signed gold discs, test pressings, and signed picture discs awaits.

Coloured discs have been a popular marketing gimmick since the 1950s and were sold as limited edition items. In the late 1970s record companies brought colour and picture discs back with a vengeance and they quickly became hot items. White, pink, orange, blue, and clear versions appeared in single form, while many were pressed on shaped vinyl.

Note: limited edition picture disc LPs such as Blondie's *Parallel Lines* or The Beatles' *Sergeant Pepper* (1978 re-release) were never intended for playing purposes as the vinyl's colour pigmentation affected sound quality.

07 *Sniffin' Glue* **punk fanzine. October 1976.** $

08 Punk/New Wave badges. Late 1970s. $

✪ **Rare records, picture disks, and coloured vinyl from the 1970s. A&M pressing of "God Save the Queen", 1977:** $$$$**; other items:** $

07

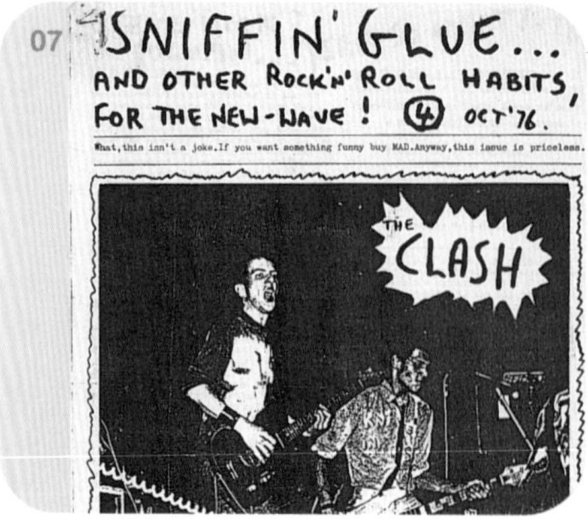

08

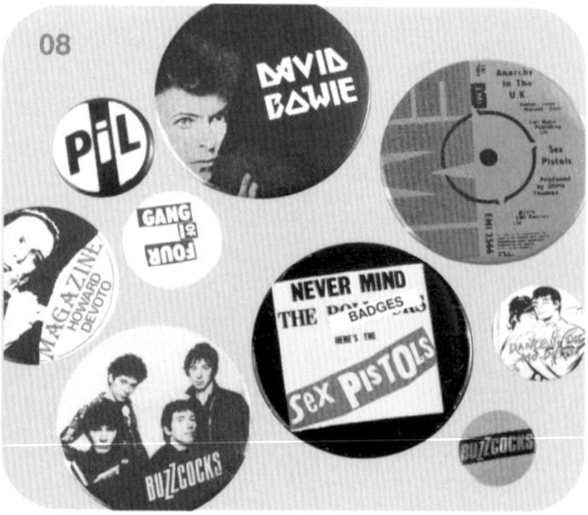

★ **coolest** buy...

SPORT SPORT SPORT S

T SPORT SPOR

PORT SPORT S

T SPORT SPOR

INTRODUCTION

Sports fans are spoilt for choice when it comes to collectibles. "The beautiful game" of soccer has an equally beautiful history, and memorabilia range from Pele shirts to Beckham boots, World Cup mascots to Subbuteo.

Sepia-remembered pitchers and sluggers embody the golden age of baseball from which bats, balls, caps, and jerseys rank among the most desirable by-products. Legions of ball game fans continue to acknowledge the heroes of the ball park with that most American of hobbies, the trading card, now also a major collectible.

Icons of the ring are helping to keep the boxing memorabilia dealers busy. Fight posters, boxing gloves, and ringside trading cards all go the distance at sports memorabilia auctions, while the name Muhammad Ali will give almost anything clout.

The breathtaking waters of surfing take us to our final arena of collecting. From Waikiki to California and beyond, the surf board best symbolizes the sport's remarkable evolution. Collectors favour Polynesian-style long boards, Hawaiian "guns", and 1970s performance boards. It's enough to make anyone want to dip their toes in the water.

SOCCER

The game we know today goes right back to the 1860s when the newly founded English Football Association helped bring together the country's disparate amateur clubs, among them Notts County and Newton Heath, the team composed of Lancashire and Yorkshire railway workers that would later become Manchester United.

Collectors of soccer memorabilia can therefore focus on a number of eras including the later Edwardian, inter-war, wartime, post-war, and modern period (post 1966 until the present).

From the modern era, the most wanted items are players' shirts, boots, and medals. The most valuable shirt has to be the one worn by Pele during the 1970 World Cup final versus Italy. Brazil samba-ed their way to an emphatic 4–1 victory, and 30 years later his shirt sold for a record £140,000.

Close behind in the list of most wanted football-related items come England 1966 shirts or medals and memorabilia connected to the game's biggest stars, past and present. David Beckham's custom Adidas Predators were sold for an amazing £13,800 ($22,080) in March 2000. Beckham-signed shirts, match balls, and photographs are also in demand, and considering his rising global profile, may prove to be sound long-term investments.

Another former red, George Best, scores highly in the memorabilia market. Best's signed number 11 Ireland shirt has traded hands for over £6,000 ($9,600), although there are many more affordable Best items around. Known in the 1960s as the "fifth Beatle" for his star quality and glamorous public profile, Best owned nightclubs and boutiques – unheard of for

01 Ball from the English Cup Final. 1903.
$ $ $ $

02 Puppet of Eric Cantona from *Spitting Image*. c.1994.
$ $ $ $

03 Signed Ian Wright shirt. c.1999. $ $

04 Drawing of Billy Meredith of Manchester United with his trademark toothpick. He was a famous agitator for a player's union (hence the money bag). c.1910. $ $ $

01

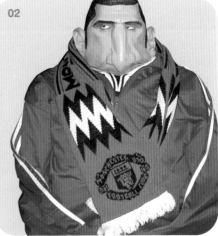

02

03

04

WILLIAM MEREDITH.
Manchester United.

a footballer of that time. For a period his image appeared on practically everything, from bedspreads to chewing gum. Best famously endorsed a brand of football boots called Stylo Matchmaker, but not all his endorsements were quite so successful. Having signed him up for a contract with a leading razor manufacturer, Best's agent was surprised to witness the player grow a thick beard.

Sadly Best never played in a World Cup. The earliest took place in Uruguay in 1930 and original tournament posters, programmes, and commemorative stamps are highly prized. For English fans 1966 was the key year. Mascot World Cup Willie appeared on anything from breakfast cereal to beer bottles, all as evocative as match tickets, programmes, or pennants.

The FA Challenge Cup began in 1872 with Bolton Wanderers beating the Royal Engineers 1–0. Memorabilia from these and other early cup clashes fetch thousands today and auction rooms can get as heated as a half-time team talk on the day itself.

05 World Cup England rosette. 1966. $

06 World Cup Willie money box. 1966. $

184-185 SOCCER

Medals from the first Wembley final of 1923 have attracted record prices, while a 1915 Cup Final programme (the last before the tournament was interrupted by World War One) is worth thousands today.

The Wembley 1966 World Cup Final programme ranks as one of the most collectible, yet others can be desirable for non-football reasons; a programme from the seemingly unmemorable 1912 Spurs vs Woolwich Arsenal match has cachet because it was in aid of the Titanic Disaster Fund.

At the more affordable end of the market are *Shoot!* annuals, completed Panini sticker albums (great for bad 1970s hairstyles), and paperback biographies. Fanzines, a phenomenon of the 1980s and 1990s, have also entered the collector's realm. The most highly collectible, and still with us today, is the irreverent *When Saturday Comes*, first published in 1986.

Some fans can take things a stage further. Condemned club grounds or stands have collectible byproducts such as wooden benches and crush barriers. Liverpool fans have bought former Anfield turnstiles, while an

The Continental game

Table soccer, babyfoot, foosball... whatever you choose to call it, the coin-op version has proved a hit with indoor players since the 1930s. Versions of the game have been manufactured in Germany, Italy, and France, the most desirable being the classic René Pierre café game from the 1950s. These are pretty hard to come by and buyers are advised to look in small French towns for them. Other vintage European makes to look out for are by Garlando and Bonzini. Although Italian-made, Bonzini's B60 is a French café institution.

enterprising Huddersfield Town supporter paid good money for Bill Shankly's dressing room toilet seat.

✪ **coolest buy** Subbuteo

Soccer nuts have been flicking to kick since 1947 when Englishman Peter Adolph brought out his now world-famous game. Original sets had cardboard teams and no playing pitch provided, but by the 1960s they were packed with "heavyweight" 3-D plastic moulded players, floodlights, and TV camera towers.

Over 300 teams were available in the peak 1970s era, the showpiece of which was the 1974 Munich World Series Edition. The most collectible Subbuteo set of all time, it comes with fencing, scoreboard, police, referee's whistle... everything except Franz Beckenbauer and Gerd Muller themselves.

Other Subbuteo collectibles include boxed teams (especially heavyweight players from the mid 1960s to early 1980s) and the 1981 Stadium Edition.

07 Panini World Cup football card. 1978. $

08 *Shoot!* annual. 1970. $

✪ Subbuteo "Continental Club Edition". Late 1960s. $

07

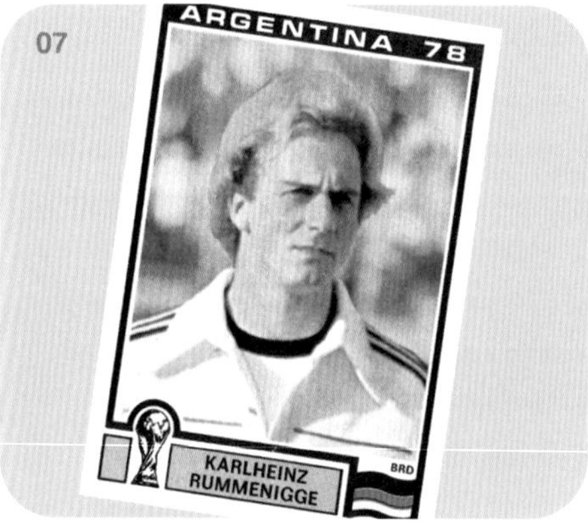

08

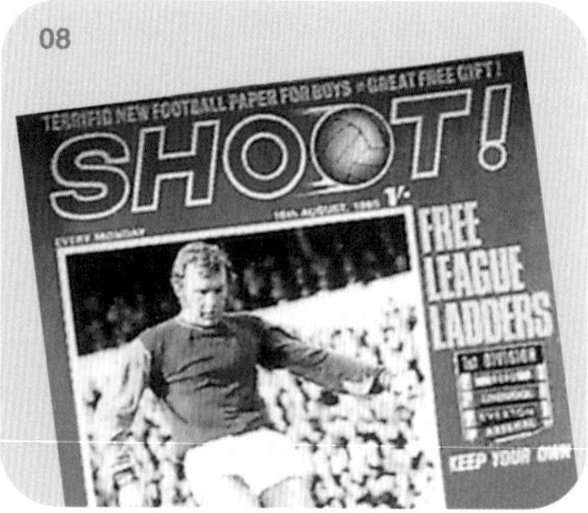

☼ **coolest** buy...

BASEBALL

As American as root beer or apple pie, baseball has been a sporting obsession for over 150 years. The first official games were played in New York, and the rules we know today were set out by the Knickerbocker Baseball Club in 1845. By the 1920s players such as New York Yankees slugger "Babe" Ruth were national heroes.

Ruth hit a record 60 home runs in 1927 yet plenty of other legends have graced the nation's ball parks and, subsequently, the Hall of Fame. In the 1950s some of the biggest names were Ted "The Kid" Williams, Willie Mays, and Mickey Mantle.

Williams was considered the greatest all-round hitter ever with a batting average of .406 in the golden year of 1941. Relics from this and other great eras are attracting crazy prices at auction, with Lou Gehrig's 1927 Yankees jersey fetching an extraordinary $305,000 ($488,000) at a recent sale.

The expression "dressed to the nines" is thought to come from the maximum nine players that a baseball team fields. Most collectible worn items include warm-up jackets, gloves, and caps. Signed items such as bats and balls generally attract the highest bids, while anything relating to a deceased Hall of Fame player tends to have higher value.

Fans can focus their collection on an infinite number of themes. Most popular are Major League teams like the Boston Red Sox from the historic Fenway Park or world-famous rivals the New York Yankees. Then there are World Series and All Star games with their accompanying match tickets, badges, and gold and diamond commemorative rings.

01 Milwaukee Brewers Co. World Series press pin. 1982. $$

02 Connie Mack comemorative game ticket (and rain check). 1944. $$

03 Baseball glove endorsed with Elmer Riddle's signature. 1930s/1940s. $$

04 Houston Astros baseball cap. 1970s. $

01

02

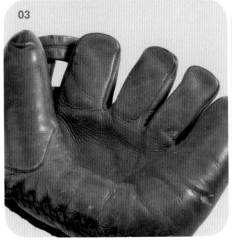

03

04

A growing collector's niche centres on the so-called Negro leagues which were formed in the late 1800s and existed right up until the 1960s. Jackie Robinson ended this long-lasting sporting apartheid when he signed for the Brooklyn Dodgers in 1947. Collectors could also look to the game played elsewhere: Japan, Mexico, and Cuba all have thriving baseball scenes.

✪ coolest buy Baseball cards

Player cards were originally promotional giveaway items given out by tobacco companies. By the 1930s the bubble gum makers took over and the hobby grew to such an extent that the cards were issued regularly. Topp's cards predominated from 1951 until the 1980s, a time when new card manufacturers helped boost the craze.

The most collectible are "rookie" cards – the first ever produced of a player always arouses most interest – while unopened packs with original packaging also have an allure.

05 Autographed photograph of Monte Irwin and Larry Doby (of the Negro League team, the Newark Eagles). 1940s. $\$$$\$$

06 Limited edition lithograph of Ted Williams by Peter Blake. $\$$$\$$

✪ Baseball trading cards; assorted publishers including Topp's and Donruss. 1960s–1980s. The set: $\$$$\$$

05

06

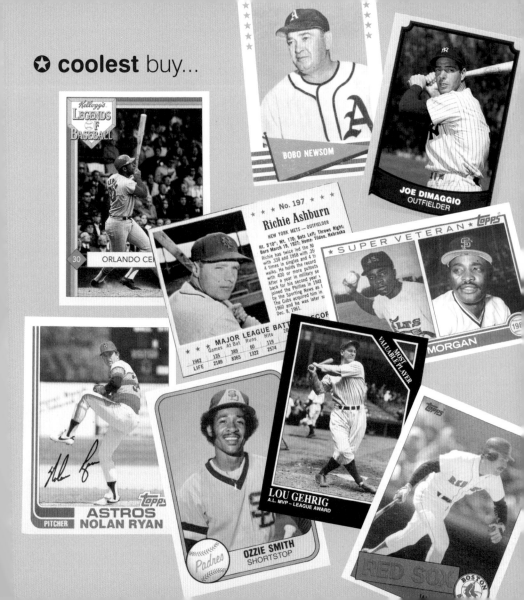

✪ **coolest** buy...

SURFING

---→

Captain James Cook was one of the first Westerners to record the sight of Hawaiian men surfing the waves on long narrow boards in the late 1700s. Unfortunately, subsequent waves of disapproving missionaries almost completely stamped out this hedonistic local activity.

Leading the Hawaiian surfing revival in the 1920s and 1930s was Duke Kahanamoku. Duke was an Olympic swimmer and sometime Hollywood actor who rode a 16ft-long board made of solid Californian redwood. He lent his name to an array of surf-related merchandise including shirts, boards, Aloha print shoes, and ukuleles. Other Hawaiiana that might interest surfing fans are traditional Polynesian woodcuts and carvings, plus prints by Eugene Savage, the artist employed by the Matson Line cruise ship company.

The most popular area of collecting, however, is vintage surfboards. These range from early 19th-century wooden planks to the foam and fibre-glass creations of the 1980s and 1990s.

American surfer Tom Blake pioneered the lighter hollow board in the 1930s, creating the first production model. Blake is considered the god-father of modern surfing; he is also credited with inventing the surfboard fin and the sailboard as well as introducing performance surfing competitions.

Long redwood boards from the 1940s and the later resin-coated balsawood boards are considered objects of rare beauty today and fetch thousands at surfing memorabilia auctions.

Styles went short in the 1970s. Some of the best examples were made by Dewey Weber or Lightning Bolt. Ben Aipa's 1973 "Stinger", featuring sting

01 Mike Diffenderfer Balsa Gun (his personal board). 8ft 9in. 1969.
$ $ $ $ $

02 Greg Noll Surf Center, shaped by Ben Aipa. 9ft 5in. 1969.
$ $ $ $

03 Lightning Bolt shaped by Reno Abellira. 7ft 4in. 1974.
$ $ $ $

04 Larry Bertlemann Hawaiian Pro Designs (his personal board). 6ft 2in. 1978.
$ $ $ $

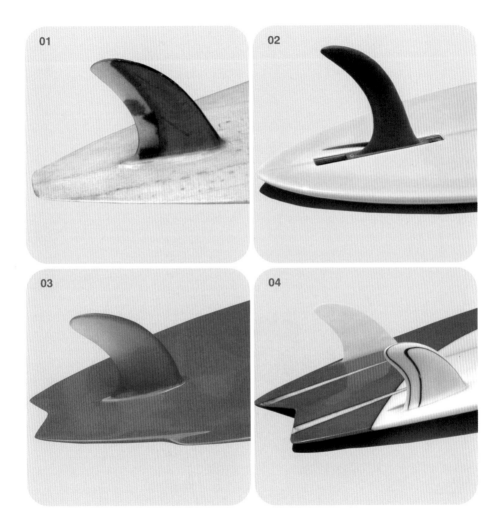

rail and swallow tail, set the style associated with 1970s riders like afro-haired Larry Bertlemann. Another rare board from this era is Gerry "Mr Pipeline" Lopez's red Lightning Bolt, which he rode in the 1976 Pipeline Masters.

Simon Anderson's three-fin "Thruster" design went on to dominate the market in the 1980s. These boards remain a good buy today, although dings (surface dents) seriously decrease their value.

✪ **coolest buy** 1960s surf culture

Bruce Brown was a keen surfer who wanted to make films about his sport. Original Bruce Brown film posters are a must for any surf fan, with the most wanted being the one for his 1966 classic, *The Endless Summer*.

The 1960s were a golden era for surf culture, and records by The Beach Boys, Dick Dale, and The Surfaris were the soundtrack to the Californian teen dream. Other highly collectible items from the era include Hawaii airline posters and back copies of *Surf Guide* and *Surfing Illustrated* magazine.

05 Eugene Savage "Aloha, Universal Word" menu cover. 1930s. [$][$]

06 Duke Kahanamoku ukelele. 1930s. [$][$]

✪ 1960s surf culture items. Film posters: [$][$]. Records: [$]

05

06

BOXING

Boxing has come a long way from the unregulated pastime that existed in early 18th-century England. Back then, pugilism was a way of settling an argument or feud, with participants able to throw, wrestle, or even jump on their opponent. The Queensberry Rules, introduced in 1743, set improved standards for the sport, and when gloves replaced the mufflers that early boxers wore for pre-fight warm ups, the sport we recognize today was born.

Legions of fighters have commanded our respect in the last few decades, notably Sugar Ray Leonard and "Iron Mike" Tyson, but none has influenced their sport, or indeed their age, in quite the way that Muhammad Ali has. He was, as he frequently reminded us, "the greatest". Ali memorabilia is without doubt the most popular genre of boxing collectible, and his most wanted items are signed Everlast gloves and hallmark Everlast white trunks (preferably signed). Fight-worn boots and robes also fetch top prices.

In 1965, Ali (then called Cassius Clay) floored challenger Sonny Liston with his infamous "phantom punch". The Neil Leifer photograph showing the victor towering menacingly over his dazed opponent is a classic sporting moment, and signed prints are among the most prized Ali pieces.

Ali memorabilia can appear from some unlikely corners; in the 1970s, US toy manufacturer Mego produced a nine-inch high Ali action figure with miniature boxing ring and sparring partner that looked suspiciously like Ken Norton. Ali has also graced the cover of countless magazines and comics.

Rocky Marciano is another collector's favourite. World Heavyweight Champion 1952–6, he remains the last undefeated title holder. His street-

01 Boxing trunks worn by Lennox Lewis when winning first heavyweight title. 1993. $$$$

02 Hand-painted Everlast boxing glove signed by Muhammad Ali. $$

03 Commemorative signed boxing glove sold at Joe Frazier vs Muhammad Ali fight. 1971.$$$$

04 Everlast boxing trunks. Recreation of trunks worn by Ali (as Cassius Clay) when he won the 1964 world title vs Sonny Liston. $$$

01

02

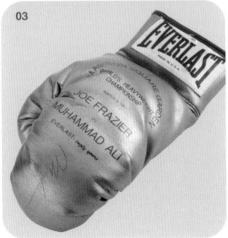

03

04

wise persona and tough training regime were the inspiration for Sylvester Stallone's Rocky Balboa character. Marciano died in a plane accident in 1969, but his image can be found on fight posters, ringside trading cards, old copies of *Ring* magazine, even a US postage stamp issued in May 1999.

The boxing memorabilia market is especially prone to fake autographs, so ask for provenance (photographic evidence of the signing or an official certificate of authenticity) when buying expensive items.

♻ **coolest buy** Boxing posters

You may not have been there, but posters from classic fights such as Ali's "Rumble In The Jungle" against George Foreman and the 1975 "Thrilla In Manila" rank as some of the boxing world's greatest treasures. Good buys can also be had with posters, programmes, or tickets that bill more contemporary fighters. A Lennox Lewis or Evander Holyfield fight poster might be cheap today, but who knows how much it could fetch in 20 years' time?

05 Rocky Marciano signature and photograph. 1964. $$$$

06 *Referee* magazine. November 1964. Signed by Muhammad Ali as Cassius Clay. $$$$

♻ Boxing posters. Lewis vs Tyson poster (2002): $. Signed Muhammad Ali site posters (dates between 1966–75): $$$$–$$$$$

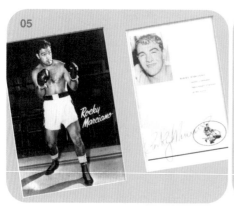

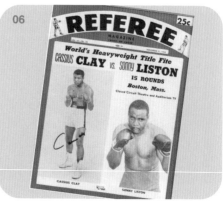

✪ **coolest** buy...

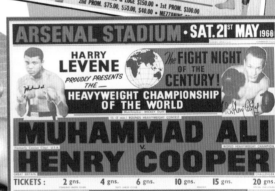

USEFUL ADDRESSES

Further information

Aero Collector magazine
PO Box 1940
Hastings
East Sussex TN34 3ZL
Tel: +44 (0)1424 440644
www.aerocollector.com

The Cantos Music Foundation
134 11th Avenue South East
Calgary, Alberta T2G 0X5
Canada
Tel: 001 403 543 5127
www.cantos.ca
*A huge collection of keyboard
instruments, from pianos to
synthesizers*

The Internet Pinball Database
www.ipdb.org
*A comprehensive listing of virtually
every pinball machine ever made*

Justin's Pinchot's Toy Rayguns
www.toyraygun.com
*A guide to toy rayguns from
around the world*

The National Football Museum
Sir Tom Finney Way
Deepdale
Preston PR1 6RU
Tel: +44 (0)1772 908 442
www.nationalfootballmuseum.
co.uk

**The National Motoring
Museum**
Beaulieu
Brockenhurst
Hampshire SO42 7ZN
Tel: +44 (0)1590 612345
www.beaulieu.co.uk

**The New England Muscle
Bicycle Museum**
www.nemusclebikes.com
*Over 120 American "muscle"
bikes from the 1960s and 1970s*

Pong-story
www.pong-story.com
*A detailed history of the Pong
videogame and its legacy*

www.RaleighChopper.info
*An information resource for the
Raleigh Chopper bicycle*

www.tvhistory.tv
*The history of TV set design,
development, and marketing*

www.vidgame.com
*A guide to videogame consoles,
games, and accessories*

www.vintagegas.com
Petrol pump globes

Vintage Guitar magazine
www.vintageguitar.com
*US-based monthly guide to
classic and collectible guitars*

Shops and dealers

**Alvin's Vintage Games
and Toys**
Tel: +44 (0)1865 772409
www.vintage-games.co.uk

American Vintage Blues
PO Box 3462
Rock Island, IL 61204-3462
USA
Tel: 001 309 721 8949
www.vintageblues.com
*Vintage denim, clothing, and
collectibles*

Andrews Cameras
17 Broad Street
Teddington
Middlesex TW11 8QZ
Tel +44 (0)20 8977 1064
www.andrewscameras.co.uk

Arcader
Tel +44 (0)15395 59235
www.arcader.co.uk
*UK-based company specializing in
supplying video arcade machines
and spares*

Bear Creek Trading
Tel +44 (0)20 7723 9848
*Baseball collectibles and
Americana*

The Board Game Company
PO Box 3633
Newport Pagnell
Bucks MK16 8XS

Tel: +44 (0)1908 611722
www.boardgamecompany.co.uk

www.boxing-memorabilia.com

Comic Book Postal Auctions
40–42 Osnaburgh Street
London NW1 3ND
Tel: +44 (0)20 7424 0007
www.compalcomics.com

Crooked Tongues
4 Ganton Street
London W1F 7QN
Tel: +44 (0)20 7494 4401
www.crookedtongues.com
Online sneaker store and resource

Cutler and Gross Vintage
7 Knightsbridge Green
London SW1X 7QL
Tel: +44 (0)20 7590 9995
www.cutlerandgross.com
*Vintage sunglasses from Cutler and
Gross and other makers*

Denim Junkies
www.denimjunkies.com
*Online vintage denim and military
clothing shop*

**Fujiyama Mama's
East-West Vintage**
**www.stores.ebay.com/Fujiyama-
Mamas-East-West-Vintage**
Online rockabilly clothing store

The Girl Can't Help It
Alfie's Antiques Market
13–25 Church Street
London NW8 8DT
Tel: +44 (0)20 7724 8984
www.alfiesantiques.com
*Vintage fashions, specializing in the
1940s and 50s*

**Hawaiian Islands Vintage
Surf Auction**
Tel: 001 808 638 7266
www.hawaiiansurfauction.com
Annual auction of Hawaiiana

Klasik.org
PO Box 8574
London E3 5UR
www.klasik.org
20th-century sunglasses

Macari's Musical Instruments
92 Charing Cross Road
London WC2H 0JB
Tel: +44 (0)20 7836 9149
www.macaris.co.uk

The Nostalgia Factory
51 North Margin Street
Boston MA 02113
USA
Tel: 001 800 479 8754
www.nostalgia.com
Original film posters and ephemera

Nostalgia Merchants
PO Box 440
Belmont, MA 02478
Tel: 001 877 652 2453 (toll free)
www.nostalgiamerchants.com
*Reproduction vintage
American bicycles*

The Pinball Heaven
302b Liverpool Rd
Southport
Merseyside PR8 4PW
Tel: +44 (0)870 746 5704
www.pinballheaven.co.uk
Pinball machines and accessories

The Pullman Gallery
14 King Street
St James's
London SWIY 6QU
Tel: +44 (0)20 7930 9595
www.pullmangallery.com
*Vintage cocktail shakers and
barware and automobilia*

Radio Days
87 Lower Marsh
London SE1 7AB
Tel: +44 (0)20 7928 0800
*Vintage clothing and 1940s–70s
memorabilia*

Rat Fink.org
www.ratfink.org
*Ed "Big Daddy" Roth T-shirts and
other merchandise*

Reckless Records
www.reckless.co.uk
www.reckless.com
*Shops selling second-hand vinyl
and CDs in London and Chicago*

The Reel Poster Gallery
72 Westbourne Grove
London W2 5SH
Tel: +44 (0)20 7727 4488
www.reelposter.com
Original film posters

Replogle Globes, Inc.
2801 South 25th Avenue
Broadview, IL 60155
USA
Tel: 001 708 343 0900
www.replogleglobes.com

Rin Tin Tin
34 North Road
Brighton BN1 1YB
Tel: +44 (0)1273 672424
Vintage and memorabilia items

RL Music
Tel: +44 (0)118 947 2474
www.rlmusic.co.uk
*Specialists in vintage
analogue synthesizers*

Rokit
225 Camden High St and
101–107 Brick Lane
London E1
www.rokit.co.uk
Vintage clothing

The Scooter Emporium
10 Dray Walk
The Old Truman Brewery
91 Brick Lane
London E1 6QL
Tel: +44 (0)20 7375 2277
www.scooteremporium.com

www.tsf1.com
Freepost (SCE8679)
Bognor Regis
West Sussex PO22 9ZT
Tel: +44 (0)870 241 2829

*Formula One and Grand Prix
merchandise, models, and
memorabilia*

20th Century Marks
12 Market Square
Westerham
Kent TN16 1AW
Tel: +44 (0)1959 562 221
www.20thcenturymarks.co.uk
Classic post-war design

**The Vintage Magazine
Company**
39–43 Brewer Street
London W1F 9UD
Tel: +44 (0)20 7439 0882
www.vinmag.com
Entertainment memorabilia

Vintage Productions, USA
Tel: 877 859 9909 (Toll free)
www.vintageproductions.com
*Militaria, specializing in the
Vietnam era*

David Webb Classic Jukeboxes
Tel: +44 (0)20 7713 7668
www.jukeboxlondon.co.uk

Zardoz Books
20 Whitecroft

Dilton Marsh
Westbury
Wiltshire BA13 4DJ
Tel: +44 (0)1373 865371
www.zardozbooks.com
*Out-of-print and collectible
fiction books*

Auction Houses

Bonhams, Chelsea
65–9 Lots Road
London SW10, UK
Tel: +44 (0)20 7393 3900
www.bonhams.com

Christie's, South Kensington
85 Old Brompton Road
London SW7 3LD
Tel: +44 (0)20 7321 3281
www.christies.com

Christie's New York
20 Rockefeller Plaza
New York, NY 10020
USA
Tel: 001 212 636 2000
www.christies.com

Onslows
The Coach House

Manor Road
Stourpaine
Dorset DT11 8TQ
Tel: +44 (0)1258 488838
www.onslows.co.uk

Sotheby's
34–35 New Bond Street
London W1A 2AA
Tel: +44 (0)20 7293 5000
www.sothebys.com

Sotheby's New York
1334 York Avenue at 72nd Street
New York, NY 10021
USA
Tel: 001 212 606 7000
www.sothebys.com

INDEX

-->

ACKNOWLEDGMENTS

Mitchell Beazley would like to acknowledge and thank all those who have helped to make this book, supplying images for publication, or allowing photography in their shops, as credited.

Key: OPG Octopus Publishing Group; photographers: IB Ian Booth, RD Roger Dixon, RS Robin Saker, TR Tim Ridley, ST Steve Tanner.

Jacket: front, above and endpaper OPG/TR/The Girl Can't Help It, below and endpaper Christie's Images; back, clockwise from top OPG/ST/The Girl Can't Help It, Reel Poster Archive Company, Anna Marie Rebus for Cantos Music Foundation, OPG/ST, OPG/ST/ Crooked Tongues.

Endpapers: front, below right © 2004 Adrienne Barr, back, above left OPG/ST/Bear Creek Trading, above right Hawaiian Islands Vintage Surf Auction, below left www.toyraygun.com, above right Hamilton Watch Co Ltd.

13: 01 OPG/Steve Tanner/20th Century Marks, 02 OPG/Tim Ridley/Boom!, 03 Bonhams, 04 www.tvhistory.tv; 14: 05, 06 OPG/Steve Tanner/20th Century Marks; 16: 07 OPG/ST/Planet Bazaar, 08 OPG/ST/Pepe Tozzo; 17: OPG/ST/20th Century Marks; 19: 01, 04 OPG/TR/Flying Duck Enterprises, 02 OPG/TR/Twenty Twenty One, 03 OPG/ST/Pepe Tozzo; 21: OPG/RS/Design Goes Pop; 23: all images from The Cocktail Shaker by Simon Khachadourian (Philip Wilson Publishers, 2000), available exclusively from The Pullman Gallery; 24: 05 OPG/TR/Flying Duck Enterprises, 06 OPG/TR/Planet Bazaar; 26: 07 OPG/TR/Flying Duck Enterprises, 08 OPG/TR/The Girl Can't Help It; 27: all OPG/ST/Rin-Tin-Tin; 29: Reel Poster Archive Company; 31: 02, 03 Reel Poster Archive Company, 04 Skinner Inc, Boston; 33: Docs Populi/Lincoln Cushing, from the archive of Alan Flatt, Oakland, CA; 35: Replogle, Inc; 37: 01, 03 OPG/ST/Zardoz Books, 38: 04, 05, 39 all: OPG/ST/Zardoz Books; 41 all, 42: 05, 06, 43: Comic Book Postal Auctions; 45: 01 OPG/RD, 02 OPG/ST/Rin-Tin-Tin, 03, 04, 47: OPG/RD; 48 all, 49: 05, 06 Robert Opie; 52: 07 OPG/Rin Tin Tin, 08 David Welch and John LaSpina; 53 right, above and below Robert Opie, left OPG/ST/David Huxtable; 59, 60: 02, 03, 62: 04, 05, 63: www.ipdb.org; 65: 01 © 2004 Adrienne Barr, 02, 03 www.pong-story.com, 04 © Intellivision Productions, Inc; 66: 05, 06 © 2004 Adrienne Barr; 67 OPG/Williams Amusements Ltd; 69, 70: 01, 02, 71, 73: OPG/Steve Tanner/Alvin's Vintage Games; 75: 01, 02 Christie's Images, 03 OPG/ST, 04 OPG/Unique Collections; 76: 05 OPG/RS/Suffolk Sci-Fi, 06 OPG/Childhood Memories; 77 above right Robert Opie, below right, above left Justin Pinchot/ www.toyraygun. com; 79: OPG/IB/Alfie's; 80: 02, 03, 81: 04 OPG/John & Simon Haley; 82: 05 OPG/Saffron Walden Saleroom, 06 OPG/TR/Alfie's; 83: Robert Opie; 85: Christie's Images; 86: 02 Christie's Images, 03 OPG/ST/Steve Tanner; 88: 03, 04, 89: Christie's Images; 95: all OPG/ST/Rokit; 96: 05 OPG/RS/20th Century Retro, 06, 97: OPG/ST/The Girl Can't Help It; 99: OPG/ST/Denim Junkies; 100: 02, 03 American Vintage Blues, www.vintageblues.com; 101: all OPG/ST/ Denim Junkies; 103: OPG/ST/Rokit; 104: 02 Lonsdale, www.lonsdale.com, 03 © Ed Roth Estate; 105 above right OPG/ST, below and centre OPG/ST/Rokit; 107: OPG/ST/Crooked Tongues; 108: 02, 03 OPG/ST/Pop Boutique; 109: OPG/ST/Crooked Tongues; 111: 01 OMEGA SA, 02 Eterna SA, 03 TAG Heuer, 04 Bonhams; 112: 05 OPG/ST/Jonathan Scatchard, 06 Hamilton Watch Co Ltd; 115: OMEGA SA, 117: 01, 04 OPG/ST/klasik.org, 02, 03 OPG/ST/Cutler & Gross; 118: 05 Rex Features/Everett Collection, 06 OPG/ST/klasik.org; 119: OPG/ST/Cutler & Gross; 120: 01, 02, 121, 122: 01, 02, 123: OPG/ST/The Girl Can't Help It; 125: 01 OPG/ST/Paul Hood, 02 OPG/ST/Laurence Corner, 03, 04 OPG/ST/Paul Hood; 126: 05 OPG/ST/Rokit, 06 Vintage Productions; 127: right OPG/ST/Paul Hood, left photo Cindy Crowell/www.stores.ebay.com/fujiyamamamaseast-westvintage; 133: 01, 03, 04 Mick Walker, 02 Beaulieu Motoring Museum; 134: 05 Mick Walker, 06 Beaulieu Motoring Museum; 136: 07, 08, 137: Mick Walker; 139 www.RaleighChopper. info; 140: 02, 03 J G Barnard, The New England Muscle Bicycle Museum, 6c Peters Road, Bloomfield, CT 06002/www.nemusclebikes.com; 141: Michael Kaplan and John Howland, Bowden Industries; 143: 01, 03 Robert Opie, 02 Beaulieu Motoring Museum, 04 Christie's Images; 144: 05, 06 www.tsf1.com; 145 courtesy Don Sherwood, www.vintagegas.com; 147: 01 Robert Opie, 02, 03 OPG/Oldnautibits, 04 OPG/T Vennet-Smith; 148: 05, 06 Robert Opie; 149: all Robert Opie; 155: 01 OPG/ST/20th Century Marks, 02 Vintage Guitar Magazine, 03, 04 Christie's Images; 156: 05 Vintage Guitar Magazine, 06 OPG; 158: 07 Christie's Images, 08 Vintage Guitar Magazine; 159: all Christie's Images; 161, 162: 02, 03; 164: 05, 05 Roland UK Ltd; 165: Anna Marie Rebus for Cantos Music Foundation; 167, 168: 02, 03, 170: 04, 05 ©Tamsyn Hill/www.juke-boxlondon.co.uk; 171 OPG/20th Century Marks; 173: 01 OPG, 02 Robert Opie, 03 OPG/IB/Christie's South Kensington, 04 OPG/Frasers; 174: 05 OPG/TR/Target Gallery; 176: 07 OPG/ST/ Bonhams, 08 OPG/ST/Giulia Hetherington; 177 above right, centre left OPG/ST/Beano's, below left, centre and right OPG/ST/Giulia Hetherington, above left OPG/ST/Pepe Tozzo; 182: all The National Football Museum, Preston; 184: 05, 06 Robert Opie; 186: 07 Panini SpA, www.paninigroup.com, 08 Robert Opie; 187: OPG/ST/Robert Opie; 189 all, 190: 05, 06, 191 all OPG/ST/Bear Creek Trading; 193: all Hawaiian Islands Vintage Surf Auction; 194: 05, 06, 195: above right, below left Hawaiian Islands Vintage Surf Auction, above left OPG/TR/Memory Lane; 197 all, 198: 05, 06, 199: OPG/ST/www.boxing-memorabilia.com.